A-LEVEL YEAR 2

AQA

Business

Topics 1.7 and 1.8

Analysing the strategic position of a business

Choosing strategic direction

Mike Pickerden

HODDER
EDUCATION
AN HACHETTE UK COMPANY

Hodder Education, an Hachette UK company, Blenheim Court, George Street, Banbury, Oxfordshire OX16 5BH

Orders

Bookpoint Ltd, 130 Park Drive, Milton Park, Abingdon, Oxfordshire OX14 4SB

tel: 01235 827827

fax: 01235 400401

e-mail: education@bookpoint.co.uk

Lines are open 9.00 a.m.–5.00 p.m., Monday to Saturday, with a 24-hour message answering service. You can also order through the Hodder Education website: www.hoddereducation.co.uk

© Mike Pickerden 2016

ISBN 978-1-4718-5673-0

First printed 2016

Impression number 5 4 3 2 1

Year 2020 2019 2018 2017 2016

This Guide has been written specifically to support students preparing for the AQA A-level Business examinations. The content has been neither approved nor endorsed by AQA and remains the sole responsibility of the author.

Typeset by Integra Software Services Pvt. Ltd., Pondicherry, India

Cover photo: Giuseppe Porzani/Fotolia

Printed in Italy

Hachette UK's policy is to use papers that are natural, renewable and recyclable products and made from wood grown in sustainable forests. The logging and manufacturing processes are expected to conform to the environmental regulations of the country of origin.

Contents

■ Getting the most from this book

Exam tips

Advice on key points in the text to help you learn and recall content, avoid pitfalls, and polish your exam technique in order to boost your grade.

Knowledge check

Rapid-fire questions throughout the Content Guidance section to check your understanding.

Knowledge check answers

1 Turn to the back of the book for the Knowledge check answers.

Summaries

■ Each core topic is rounded off by a bullet-list summary for quick-check reference of what you need to know.

Exam-style questions

Commentary on the questions

Tips on what you need to do to gain full marks, indicated by the icon **e**

Sample student answers

Practise the questions, then look at the student answers that follow.

Questions & Answers

(a) Explain how Carroll's corporate social responsibility pyramid can be applied to IKEA. [6 marks]

e When a question asks you about a particular theory or concept, it is a good idea to start your answer with a definition of the theory/concept. A maximum of two arguments is sufficient for 6-mark questions.

(b) Analyse the importance of globalisation for a business such as IKEA. [9 marks]

e Remember that 'analysis' questions require you to make a well-developed line of argument for each point made. To gain 'application' marks you must support your argument with relevant data and/or data from the case study. There is no need to consider both sides of the argument and/or write a conclusion as this question would not have any marks for evaluation.

(c) To what extent do you think corporate social responsibility has been the main reason for IKEA's sales growth? [16 marks]

e The phrase 'To what extent' is commonly used for evaluation questions. Remember that these questions will require you to make arguments for and against followed by a supported judgement.

Student A

(a) Carroll's social responsibility pyramid shows the different stages that a business has to achieve in order to be considered a socially responsible business. IKEA has achieved all of these stages as firstly it has achieved its economic responsibilities by operating as a profitable business. This can be shown by achieving sales of £23 billion in 2015.

Secondly, it has achieved its legal responsibilities by meeting the legal requirements of each country that it operates in. For example, it has recently announced that all its UK workers will be paid the 'living wage' of at least £7.85 per hour. Thirdly, IKEA has met its ethical responsibilities through its policy of social responsibility, which means it treats all of its stakeholders well.

Finally, IKEA has achieved its philanthropic responsibilities through the Kamprad Family Foundation, which aims to donate £20 million each year to 'support, stimulate and reward education and scientific research in a way promoting entrepreneurship, environment, competence, health and social progress'.

e 6/6 marks awarded. This answer reveals good understanding of Carroll's social responsibility model and provides relevant illustrations of how IKEA achieves it.

Student B

(a) This is a pyramid that shows what a business needs to do if it is to be socially responsible. It includes economic, legal and ethical.

IKEA is socially responsible because it makes good sales and profits. It also treats its employees well by paying them the 'living wage'.

76 AQA Business

Commentary on sample student answers

Read the comments (preceded by the icon **e**) showing how many marks each answer would be awarded in the exam and exactly where marks are gained or lost.

■ About this book

This Student Guide 3, along with its companion (Student Guide 4), has been written with one thing in mind: to provide you with the ideal resource for your revision of the second year of the AQA Business A-level. The topics covered in this guide build upon the knowledge gained during the first year of the AQA Business A-level.

In your study of the subject you will look at business in a variety of contexts, small and large, national and global, service and manufacturing.

The overall focus of the second year of the AQA Business A-level is analysing the strategic position of a business, choosing strategic direction, assessing strategic methods and managing strategic change. The study of strategic decision making builds on the study of decision making in the functional areas in the first year of the AQA Business A-level.

Central to this specification are the following themes:
- The impact of technology on strategic decision making
- The influences of corporate social responsibility, ethical and environmental issues on strategic decisions
- The difficulties in forecasting trends
- The importance of assessing feasibility and risk when making strategic decisions
- The impact on stakeholders of strategic decisions and their response to such decisions.

The focus of Book 3 is the following:
- Analysing the strategic position of a business
- Choosing strategic direction.

The Content Guidance section offers concise coverage combining an overview of key terms and concepts with identification of opportunities for you to illustrate higher-level skills of analysis and evaluation. Read through the topic area before attempting a question from the Questions & Answers section.

The Questions & Answers section gives examples of the various types of questions that you are likely to be faced with: multiple choice, short-answer questions, data response, a case study (based upon the content of Book 3) and essay questions. The multiple-choice and short-answer questions focus on the broad content of this book and the data-response questions focus on specific aspects of content.

A common problem for students and teachers is the lack of resources, and in particular exam-style questions that cover individual areas of study. The questions in this guide are tailored so that you can apply your learning while the topic is still fresh in your mind, either during the course itself or when you have revised a topic in preparation for the examination. Along with the sample answers, this should give you a sound basis for sitting your exams in business.

Content Guidance

■ Analysing the strategic position of a business

Mission, corporate objectives and strategy

Influences on the mission of a business

A **mission statement** is an attempt by a business to put its **aims** into words that will motivate its employees to work towards achieving those aims. It should give employees a sense of direction and ensure that all functional areas of the business are working together in order to achieve the same goal.

Influences on the mission of a business can include:

- Purpose – the reason why the business exists. This could be what the founders aimed to achieve when they started the business. For example, Mark Zuckerberg, founder of Facebook, wanted to 'make the world more open and connected'.
- Values – what the company believes in. This is often linked to business ethics and how the business treats its various stakeholders such as employees, customers and suppliers.
- Standards and behaviour – how employees are expected to behave. This is linked to the culture of the business. It is set by the senior management regarding what they require from employees in terms of working hours, dress code and interaction with other workers.
- Strategy – the competitive position of the company. Strategy is the medium- to long-term plans the business needs in order to achieve its objectives.

Internal and external influences on corporate objectives and decisions

An **objective** is a goal or target that a business wishes to achieve. It should be SMART. For example: 'To achieve a 5% increase in market share of the computer game market by 2020.'

Internal influences include:

- The ambitions of the chief executive – this is often linked to the personality and leadership style of the chief executive. Successful leaders will often set challenging objectives and inspire their employees to achieve them.
- The financial position of the business – the profitability and cash flow position of a business are important factors when deciding upon objectives. For example, a profitable business will be in a strong position to afford the investment required in order to achieve ambitious objectives.

Mission statement
An attempt to put the corporate aims of a business into words that inspire.

Aims Generalised statements of where the business is heading, from which specific objectives can be set.

Knowledge check 1

Write down three typical business aims.

Objectives The goals a business sets that need to be achieved to keep the business on track to achieve its aims.

Knowledge check 2

What does the acronym SMART stand for?

- Human resources in terms of the quality and ability of senior staff – a business will need highly skilled and experienced managers in order to successfully carry out the strategy required to achieve objectives.

External influences include:
- Competition – how competitive the market is in which the business is operating. If a business is competing against strong rivals, it may need to set less ambitious objectives.
- Changes in consumer tastes – if the business's product/service loses popularity, the business will need to set different objectives, such as developing new products.
- The economic environment – if the economy becomes stronger, consumers will be more confident and increase their spending. This could enable a business to set more ambitious objectives.
- Changes in legislation – this could make achieving objectives more difficult. For example, if the government raised the minimum wage, the increase in costs might make it more difficult for a business to achieve profit objectives.
- Pressure from shareholders – does the business adopt a 'short-termist' approach? In this case the business may have to set an objective of maximising its profits in order to provide shareholders with higher dividend payments.
- Type of business ownership – private or public limited company, non-profit organisation, public or private sector? Public limited companies will set objectives linked to ensuring that shareholders are satisfied, whereas a non-profit organisation may set objectives linked to social values.

The distinction between strategy and tactics

Once a business has decided upon its objectives, it then has to formulate a **strategy**, as well as the **tactics** required. Strategic decisions tend to be medium or long term. For example, in order to achieve the objective of increasing its market share to 20% by 2020, a business may decide upon a strategy of targeting a new market segment. The tactical decisions will be short term, for example using an advertising campaign aimed at this market segment.

The links between mission, corporate objectives and strategy

Figure 1 The chain from mission to strategy

Figure 1 shows the logic chain from mission to strategy.

Strategy The medium-to long-term plan that the business needs in order to achieve its objectives.

Tactics Responses to short-term opportunities or

The impact of strategic decision making on functional decision making

Strategic decisions influence each functional area of the business, specifically marketing, finance, human resources and operations.

Each functional area will be set a specific objective. The achievement of this objective contributes to achieving the corporate objective set by the business. In order to achieve its objective, each functional area has to decide upon the best strategy and tactics.

It is important that each functional area coordinates with the others in order to achieve its objective. For example, if a business has decided upon a strategy of launching its products into an overseas market:

- The marketing department would be responsible for activities such as market research, sales forecasting and the marketing campaign.
- The operations department would need to organise the additional production required as well as the storage and distribution.
- The human resources department would need to recruit staff with specialist knowledge of the overseas market, as well as provide training for existing staff.
- The finance department would need to provide the necessary funds and set a budget for each of the other functions.

Knowledge check 4

Name one functional objective for each of the following areas:

- finance
- marketing
- operations
- human resources.

The value of SWOT analysis

SWOT analysis is a decision-making tool used by senior managers to gain an insight into the current and potential position of a business. It gives them the evidence to help decide future strategy.

It is important that businesses regularly conduct SWOT analysis as a basis for making strategic decisions. This requires regular market research to assess the external environment as well as constant reviews of internal performance.

Knowledge check 5

Think of one advantage and one disadvantage resulting from the use of SWOT analysis.

Exam tip

When answering questions on this topic, always consider the external environment that the business is facing in the case study, for example how competitive is the market or state of the economy? Ask yourself whether the objectives and strategy are appropriate in order to achieve the aims expressed in the mission statement.

SWOT S = Strengths; W = Weaknesses; O = Opportunities; T = Threats. Strengths and weaknesses are internal. Opportunities and threats are external.

Summary

In this section you need to be able to:

- Understand what the purpose of a mission statement is.
- Define a business aim.
- Name three typical corporate objectives.
- Name two internal and two external influences on a corporate objective.
- Appreciate why corporate objectives must be SMART.
- Define corporate strategy.
- Understand the difference between strategic and tactical decisions.
- Draw a flow diagram that shows the link between a company's mission, corporate objectives and strategy.
- Define functional objectives.
- Explain how the achievement of a functional objective contributes to achieving a corporate objective.
- Understand the benefit to a business of conducting a SWOT analysis.

Financial ratio analysis

Balance sheets

The function of accounting is to provide information to various stakeholder groups regarding how well the business is performing financially. Key stakeholders who would be interested in the financial performance include shareholders, employees and suppliers. The key information they require is obtained from the **balance sheet** and the **income statement**. Table 1 shows a simplified balance sheet while Table 2 is an example of a fuller version and Table 3 is a completed balance sheet.

Knowledge check 6

Think of one reason why the following stakeholders would be interested in the financial performance of a business:

- Shareholders
- Employees
- Suppliers

Table 1 A simplified balance sheet

Spark plc: Simplified vertical balance sheet	
	£
Long-term (non-current) assets	300,000
Short-term (current) assets	100,000
Total assets	400,000
Balancing with: Total capital	400,000

A business owns assets. These can be either non-current or current. Non-current assets last for more than 12 months. They include items such as property, vehicles and machinery. Current assets last for less than 12 months. They include cash, inventories and receivables.

A business will have current liabilities. These are items that have to be paid within 12 months. They include items such as a bank overdraft and payables. The liquidity of a business can be calculated by subtracting current liabilities from current assets.

Balance sheet Shows an organisation's assets and liabilities at a precise point in time. The balance sheet shows what the business owns and what it owes at a certain point in time.

Income statement Records the amount of profit (or loss) that a business has made over a previous trading period.

Exam tip

Remember that in a balance sheet figures for liabilities are in brackets because they represent a negative figure.

This figure is known as working capital. The business can also calculate the value of its assets employed by adding together non-current assets and **working capital**. **Assets employed** represents what the business is worth at a particular point in time. To pay for its assets employed a business needs capital. Capital represents what the business owes.

Working capital = current assets – current liabilities

Assets employed = non-current assets + working capital

Table 2 A fuller version of a balance sheet

Spark plc: Fuller version of the firm's balance sheet	
	£
Property	180,000
Machinery and vehicles	120,000
Inventories	80,000
Receivables and cash	60,000
Current liabilities	(40,000)
Assets employed	400,000
Total capital	400,000

Capital consists of non-current liabilities – these are long-term loans that are paid back over a period greater than 12 months. Subtracting non-current liabilities (loan capital) from assets employed, the business can calculate the value of its net assets. Net assets are financed by both:

- share capital – funds raised from selling shares, and
- reserves – reinvested profits.

Share capital and reserves are known as 'total equity'.

The capital employed figure represents how the business has financed its assets employed. In order to balance, assets employed must always be equal to capital employed.

    Total equity + non-current liabilities = capital employed

Knowledge check 7

What is the difference between non-current and current assets?

Table 3 A complete version of a balance sheet

Spark plc: Balance sheet for 31 December last year		
	£	£
Property	180,000	
Machinery and vehicles	120,000	300,000
Inventories	80,000	
Receivables and cash	60,000	
Current liabilities	(40,000)	
Total assets less current liabilities		400,000
Loan capital		(250,000)
Net assets		150,000
Share capital	50,000	
Reserves	100,000	
Total equity		150,000

Income statements

The income statement records all the business's revenue and costs within a given trading period. While a balance sheet can be drawn up at a particular point in time, the income statement records what has happened during a previous period of time, usually the past 6 or 12 months.

Figure 2 sets out the basic structure of an income statement for a public limited company.

		£m
	Revenue	26.0
less	Cost of sales	(17.0)
gives	Gross profit	9.0
less	Overheads	(4.0)
gives	Operating profit	5.0
less	Financing costs	1.5*
gives	Profit before taxation	6.5
less	Tax	(2.0)
gives	Profit after taxation for the year	4.5

*In this case more interest was earned than paid out

Figure 2 The basic structure of an income statement

The income statement consists of four main stages:

1 **Gross profit** – calculated by subtracting cost of sales from revenue.
2 **Operating profit** – calculated by subtracting overheads from gross profit.
3 **Profit before tax** – calculated by subtracting financing costs from operating profit.
4 **Profit after tax** – calculated by subtracting tax from profit before tax.

Profit after tax is also known as 'earnings'. Earnings can be either distributed or retained. The directors of the business have to decide what proportion of the earnings should be given to the shareholders as **dividends**. It is important to give shareholders dividend payments as they are the owners of the business and have the power to sack the directors if they are not happy with the business's performance. However, the directors also need to retain some of the earnings as these funds are needed for future investment. Without sufficient investment, the business's performance may suffer in the long term.

Knowledge check 11

Think of three items a business could invest in that may lead to improved long-term performance.

Exam tip

In an exam, you may be given a balance sheet and income statement as part of a case study or data-response question. Often there will be additional information which may explain some of the figures. Remember to use this information, as well as the actual figures, when answering questions on the financial performance of the business. For example, if there is a big difference between gross and operating profit, there may be information in the case study about why the overheads have increased.

Exam tip

Remember that negative figures in an income statement are always in brackets.

Gross profit = sales revenue – cost of sales

Knowledge check 8

What does 'cost of sales' represent?

Operating profit = gross profit – overheads

Knowledge check 9

What are 'overheads'?

Profit before tax = operating profit – financing costs

Knowledge check 10

What are 'financing costs'?

Profit after tax = profit before tax – tax

Dividends Represent the share of the profit after tax given to shareholders.

Financial ratio analysis

The function of accounting is to provide stakeholders with financial information about how the business has performed over a certain period of time. The technique used to provide this information is known as **ratio analysis**.

To analyse company accounts, a well-ordered and structured approach needs to be followed. Table 4 outlines the seven-point approach to ratio analysis.

> **Ratio analysis** An examination of accounting data by relating one figure to another.

Table 4 The seven-point approach to ratio analysis

The investigation process		
Step 1	Reason	The starting point for interpreting financial accounts is establishing why you are doing so. If you are considering supplying a company with a large order of goods, you want to try to establish its financial stability and ability to pay.
Step 2	Identification	Identify the relevant figures from the financial accounts.
Step 3	Process	Decide what method(s) of analysis will provide you with the most useful and meaningful results.
Step 4	Calculation	Make a comparison between data by calculating one figure as a ratio of another. For example, profit as a percentage of sales revenue or borrowings as a proportion of total capital.
Step 5	Comparison	Compare the figures from this period with the results from the last period, those of your competitors or other companies under investigation.
Step 6	Interpretation	Look at the results obtained and interpret them in relation to values that would be considered poor, average or good.
Step 7	Action	If certain results are worrying, initiate further investigation (maybe into areas which are not covered in the financial accounts), or take corrective action.

The main types of ratios are:

- **Profitability ratios**. These measure the relationship between gross/net profit and revenue, assets and capital employed. Return on capital employed is an important profitability ratio.
- **Liquidity ratios**. These investigate the short-term financial stability of a firm by examining whether there are sufficient short-term assets to meet the short-term liabilities (debts). The current ratio is an important liquidity ratio.
- **Gearing**. This examines the extent to which the business is dependent upon borrowed money; it is concerned with the long-term financial position of the company.
- **Efficiency ratios**. These measure how efficiently an organisation uses its resources and controls credit. Payables days, receivables days and inventory turnover are important efficiency ratios (see below).

Profitability

Profit margins compare the amount of profit made in relation to sales revenue. The two key profit margins are gross profit margin and operating profit margin, which are covered in Student Guide 2: Topics 1.4–1.6.

$$\text{Return on capital employed (ROCE)} = \frac{\text{operating profit}}{\text{capital employed}} \times 100$$

This ratio measures the efficiency with which the firm generates profit from the funds invested in the business.

> **Knowledge check 12**
>
> How do you calculate operating profit and capital employed?

The higher the value of ROCE, the better, as a high and rising figure indicates that resources are being used efficiently. High ROCE will please shareholders as they should benefit from improved profitability through increased dividends and a rising share price. ROCE needs to be compared with:

■ previous years – to see whether it has improved
■ competitors – to see how well the business is performing against its rivals
■ interest rates offered by banks – is the business generating better returns to investors compared with putting money into a savings account?

Liquidity

Liquidity is concerned with working capital and how it is being managed. Too little working capital indicates that the business may struggle to pay all its debts and could face a cash-flow problem. Too much working capital indicates that the business may not be making the most efficient use of its financial resources.

$$\text{Current ratio} = \frac{\text{current assets}}{\text{current liabilities}}$$

It is usually expressed as a ratio, for example 2:1.

Example

Bannam Ltd has current assets of £30,000 and current liabilities of £10,000:

Current ratio = current assets : current liabilities

$$= £30,000 : £10,000$$

$$= 3 : 1$$

Current ratio = 3:1

A ratio of 3:1 indicates that a business has £3 of current assets for every £1 of current liabilities.

Accountants recommend that the 'ideal' current ratio should be between 1.5:1 and 2:1. This means that the business can comfortably pay its short-term debts, but does not have too much tied up in unproductive resources.

Gearing

Gearing measures the financial stability of a business. It shows how reliant it is upon borrowed money.

$$\text{Gearing} = \frac{\text{non-current liabilities}}{\text{capital employed}} \times 100$$

If a business has a gearing ratio of above 50% it is said to be highly geared. This means that more than 50% of its capital employed is provided by loans. This means that the business has to pay interest on its loans before it can pay dividends and/ or reinvest profits. High gearing indicates high risk. Lower geared businesses are considered lower risk and may be able to negotiate loans more easily.

Efficiency

These ratios measure how well a business manages its resources.

Exam tip

The current ratio can vary according to the type of business. For example, businesses that hold inventory that can be sold off quickly, such as supermarkets, can operate with much lower current ratios than manufacturing firms, which may struggle to sell their inventory quickly. In an exam, always consider the type of business featured in the question when interpreting its current ratio.

Inventory turnover measures the number of times in a year a business sells and replaces its inventory.

$$\text{Inventory turnover} = \frac{\text{cost of sales}}{\text{inventories}}$$

It is expressed in number of times per year.

Inventory turnover is a good indicator of liquidity as it shows how quickly the business is selling its products. This ratio is highly dependent upon the type of business in terms of the product sold and inventory. For example, a business that sells products that are perishable, such as a florist, would expect to sell and replace its inventory on a daily basis. This means that it would have a high inventory turnover. In contrast, a car dealer may sell only a few cars a week and could have a car in its showroom for several months, resulting in a lower inventory turnover.

Receivables days shows how long on average it takes for a business to receive payment from its customers.

$$\text{Receivables days} = \frac{\text{receivables}}{\text{revenue}} \times 365$$

It is usually expressed in days.

Receivables days is often linked to how much trade credit a business gives its customers. Consequently, it is a useful measure of liquidity. The shorter the receivables days figure, the quicker a business is receiving payment from its customers.

Payables days shows how long a business takes to pay its suppliers on average.

$$\text{Payables days} = \frac{\text{payables}}{\text{cost of sales}} \times 365$$

It is usually expressed in days.

The difference between receivables and payables days is a good indicator of how efficiently a business is managing its working capital. Receivables days should always be shorter than payables days. A business must be careful when deciding how long it will take before paying its suppliers. While longer payables days is good for liquidity, it may damage the relationship with suppliers if they have to wait a long time before getting paid.

Knowledge check 15

Identify one way a car dealer could improve its inventory turnover.

Knowledge check 16

Identify and explain one way a business could improve its receivables days.

Knowledge check 17

What problems might result for a business from an increase in its payables days?

Exam tip

In an exam you may be given financial data for two consecutive years. It is important that you calculate relevant ratios for both years and make a comparison. Alternatively, you may be given the ratio figures for a competitor. In this case it is important that you compare your ratio calculations with these figures. Remember to always show your workings when completing ratio calculations.

The value of financial ratios when assessing performance

Analysing ratios over time is useful because it enables stakeholders to compare different years and identify whether financial performance has improved or worsened (Table 5). It highlights the areas where the business has to improve and enables managers to identify the reasons for poor performance, in order to develop the strategies needed.

Table 5 Ratio trends

Ratio trend over time	Example	Implications
Falling current ratio	1.4 two years ago; 0.9 last year; 0.6 this year	Worryingly sharp fall in liquidity; needs to be tackled immediately, e.g. through a **rights issue**
Rising receivables days	42 two years ago; 48 last year; 59 this year	Customers are taking significantly longer to pay, which will drain your own cash holdings and therefore hit liquidity
Falling gearing	52% two years ago; 48% last year; 40% this year	Gearing has dropped from being a bit too high/risky to being normal/safer
Falling ROCE	34% two years ago; 23% last year; 14% this year	Dramatic fall in profitability, perhaps because competitors have caught you up; you've lost your competitive advantage

However, most published accounts provide data covering only the most recent two years. Trends over at least three years should be considered.

Analysing ratios in comparison with similar businesses is also valuable. It enables the business to identify its strengths and weaknesses compared with its rivals. For example, consider the comparison between Supergroup and Ted Baker shown in Table 6.

Table 6 Comparative ratios between Supergroup and Ted Baker

Ratio	Supergroup plc 26 April 2014	Ted Baker plc 25 January 2014	Conclusions
Gross margins	59.7%	61.7%	Very similar, with Ted Baker achieving slightly higher value added
Operating margins	14.3%	12.3%	Supergroup's slight superiority suggests its overheads are lower than Ted Baker's
Return on capital	21.0%	35.3%	Ted Baker's remarkable figures show efficient use of its invested long-term capital
Inventory turnover	2.23 times	1.53 times	Both are remarkably slow (for fashion clothing firms) but Supergroup is better
Payables (days)	123.8 days	133.9 days	Both very slow, again; suppliers have to wait 4 months+ to be paid

Limitations of financial ratios

1 They do not consider qualitative information – such as brand image, business culture, quality of the workforce – which is difficult to measure but can play a significant part in overall performance.

2 Accounts are historical and therefore cannot be used as a guide for future performance. This is particularly true in rapidly changing markets such as fashion and technology.

3 A business may 'window dress' its accounts to make the financial performance appear better than it actually is, for example by overvaluation of assets.

Exam tip

In a case study or data-response question, always look for information that may provide the reasons behind the ratio analysis figures. Remember, this information is often qualitative. For example, an increase in ROCE could be due to an inspirational leader who has motivated the workforce, resulting in higher sales revenue and improved financial efficiency.

Knowledge check 18

Why would managers of a business wish to 'window dress' the accounts?

Summary

In this section you should be able to:
- Understand how a balance sheet is constructed.
- Work out working capital, assets employed and capital employed.
- Understand the difference between gross and operating profit.
- Identify which stakeholders are interested in the financial performance of a business and explain the reasons why.
- Know the difference between profitability, liquidity, gearing and efficiency ratios.
- Remember the formulae for ROCE, current ratio, gearing, inventory turnover, receivables days and payables days.
- Understand the significance of your ratio analysis calculations in terms of their causes and possible effects for that particular business.
- Identify information in the case study/data-response material that could offer an explanation for the financial ratios.
- Appreciate the benefits and limitations of ratio analysis when assessing business performance.

Overall performance

How to analyse data other than financial statements

Public limited companies have a legal obligation to publish details regarding their financial performance. While this is valuable, it does not provide a complete picture of the overall performance of the business. Financial ratios give useful indicators of financial performance, but investigation into the reasons behind these figures is often related to the other functional areas of the business, specifically marketing, human resources and operations.

Marketing measures of performance

Market share is the most commonly used measure of marketing performance as it reveals the sales of the business's products in comparison with those of its rivals. Market share is also directly related to the sales revenue of the business.

Market share directly measures the performance of the marketing department. But what marketing activities contribute to a gain in market share? The following are all useful performance indicators:

- **Brand image.** Does this enable the business to retain existing customers as well as attract new ones?
- **Customer service.** The business needs to ensure that it records all customer complaints and takes steps to reduce them.
- **Effectiveness of marketing campaigns.** Market research should be carried out before, during and after a marketing campaign in order to measure whether it has achieved its objectives.
- **New product sales as a percentage of all product sales.** The launch of new products is crucial for long-term success, particularly in fast-changing markets characterised by products with short product life cycles.

Human resource measures of performance

'The most important asset of a business is its employees.' Chief executives will often make declarations similar to this when commenting upon business performance. All

Knowledge check 19

What is the formula for market share?

Knowledge check 20

How could the marketing department measure the success of a marketing campaign based upon digital media?

businesses should keep quantitative information on the performance of their employees. You have already learned about the following measures of employee performance:

- labour turnover and retention
- labour productivity
- employee costs as percentage of turnover
- labour cost per unit.

A 'hard' human resource approach places great emphasis on direct measurement of employee performance. In this environment employees are closely monitored to ensure that they work at optimum efficiency. However, this approach has been criticised for creating extra stress on employees, resulting in low morale. Also there are many jobs which are hard to directly measure in terms of employee performance – for example, how easy is it to measure the performance of a doctor or a software developer?

Businesses that adopt a 'soft' human resource approach are more likely to measure employee performance in terms of how satisfied employees are in working for them. Typical measurements may include:

- annual ratings of staff satisfaction
- amount spent on training per employee
- statistics relating to the composition of the workforce regarding gender, ethnic background and disabled employees.

Operations measures of performance

There are a number of different measures of operational performance which you will already have studied. These include:

- capacity utilisation
- quality
- productivity
- speed of response and flexibility.

Table 7 Measures of operational performance

Areas of operations	Detailed measures
1. Managing quality	Cutting customer returns from 5% to 2% In 2014 the US JD Power survey of vehicle dependability placed Lexus first (by a large margin) and the BMW Mini last
2. Managing waste	In 2013/14 Tesco counted its annual food waste at 56,580 tonnes; it plans to report each year on how well it is doing compared with that starting point
3. Productivity	Sales per square ft. (Sainsbury's, sales per square foot down from £20.42 in 2010 to £18.93 in 2014) Output per worker (at JLR, cars per worker per year have increased from 14 in 2011 to 15.53 in 2014)
4. Managing time	At Panetteria Italiana the production time for making then baking bread has shortened from 5hrs to 4hrs At Virgin Rail, 81.2% of trains arrived within 10 minutes of their scheduled arrival time in October-November 2014
5. Managing growth	Capital investment (at JLR, investment spending has jumped from £900 million in 2011 to £2,680 million in 2014)

Measuring operational performance is critical for business success (Table 7). A business that achieves high levels of capacity utilisation may benefit from lower unit costs because fixed costs are spread over more units. Lower unit costs enable the business to

Knowledge check 21

What are the formulae for calculating labour turnover and labour productivity?

Knowledge check 22

Identify three ways employees can contribute to improved business performance.

Knowledge check 23

What is the formula for capacity utilisation?

either reduce prices, which could lead to increased sales, or keep the price the same but make a greater profit margin on each product sold.

A business that achieves consistently high quality will gain a good reputation. This could lead to brand loyalty and make demand more price inelastic due to the fact that customers are prepared to pay higher prices for good quality. This enables the business to add value to its products and services.

Exam tip

Financial performance is directly linked to the performance of the other functional areas. In a data response/case study, always try to link the data provided for marketing, human resources and operations to financial indicators such as profitability and liquidity.

The importance of core competencies

Core competences are often the reason for the long-term success of a business.

Businesses can develop expertise in a range of functional areas. This can give them a unique selling point (USP) compared with their competitors. For example, luxury car companies such as BMW and Mercedes have developed a reputation for well-designed, reliable and high-quality cars. Consequently, these businesses have enjoyed high market shares in the luxury car market for a considerable period of time. This expertise is due to great emphasis upon recruiting and training highly skilled engineers and designers that has been built up over a long period of time. Toyota, through the launch of its 'Lexus' range of luxury cars, has tried to compete with BMW and Mercedes for many years, but has had only limited success. This is due partly to the fact that Toyota has struggled to develop the same core competences. The development of core competences can be directly linked to the culture and the leadership of the business.

Assessing short- and long-term performance

Short- and long-term performance is linked to the time scale in which a business's performance is measured.

Short-term performance is concerned with measuring immediate issues. This approach is known as short termism. Many UK businesses have been criticised for adopting a short-termist approach as it leads to:
- insufficient spending on research and development
- greater emphasis on providing shareholders with high dividends rather than retaining profit for investment
- achieving growth through taking over other businesses rather than through organic growth.

The most common reason why a business adopts a short-term approach is the pressure from the financial markets. The majority of shares in UK public limited companies are owned by pension funds rather than private shareholders. The performance of pension fund managers is measured every 3 months, so consequently they are under pressure to deliver improved results. This means that pension fund managers will in turn put pressure on the directors of the business to generate high returns for shareholders.

Knowledge check 24

How does positive operational performance contribute to an improvement in ROCE for a business?

Core competences The fundamental learnings within the business that give it its inner strength within its particular expertise. They provide the source of its competitive advantage.

Knowledge check 25

What do you consider are the core competences of a company such as Apple?

Short term The time scale within which decisions can be reversed without causing too much damage.

Long term A time scale in which resource commitments make it hard to back down.

Knowledge check 26

What is the potential danger for a business if it focuses just on keeping shareholders happy by giving them high dividends?

Long-term performance is measured over a time frame of between 5 and 10 years. It is often linked to strategies such as entering new markets or developing new products. It is argued that private limited companies (ltd) can adopt a more long-term approach as the majority of their shares are owned by private individuals rather than by pension funds. Many ltds are small to medium-sized family-owned firms. This means that they are under less pressure to deliver immediate improvements in results.

A long-term approach means that the business will retain more profits for investment in areas such as:

■ research and development
■ staff training
■ new machinery and technology.

The success of the **Mittelstand** in Germany is often cited as an example of the benefits of a long-term approach.

These businesses concentrate on developing specific activities very well. This is linked to the concept of core competences discussed earlier. As a result, Germany has 20 times more businesses that are 'world market leaders' than the UK does (see Figure 3 and Table 8).

Mittelstand The business sector in Germany that is dominated by medium-sized family-owned and run businesses.

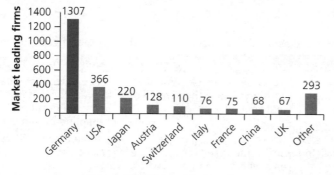

Figure 3 World market leaders

Knowledge check 27

Why might a long-term approach upset shareholders?

Table 8 The British versus the German business model

	Plc	Mittelstand
Typical financial structure	Strong equity base Moderate gearing	Strong equity base Moderate gearing
Typical ownership structure	Owned by many, relatively small shareholders	Family-owned or majority family-owned with some shares listed on the stock market
Typical approach to spending on R&D and trainee staff	Varies, but many will look for a low-spend model with high levels of outsourcing (and low investment in staff)	Desire for very long-term success and a sense of moral duty creates a culture of investment in people and technology
Typical business objectives	Maximise short-term share price to keep the market happy, and to enjoy a big bonus due to the high share price	Maintain a world-leading position to hand over a continuingly successful business to the next generation

The value of different measures of assessing business performance

Business performance measures how well the company has done in meeting its objectives. Traditionally, profitability has been the key measurement of business performance. More recently, businesses have realised that non-financial measures of performance are becoming increasingly important. Two commonly used measures are Kaplan and Norton's balanced scorecard model and Elkington's triple bottom line.

Kaplan and Norton's balanced scorecard

The **financial perspective** is concerned with business performance in terms of profit growth, return on capital and liquidity. The **customer perspective**, meanwhile, measures performance in terms of customer satisfaction. Measures such as market share, rate of repeat purchase and customer satisfaction surveys are commonly used. The **business process perspective** focuses on the operational performance. Measures include productivity, quality and speed of response. The **learning and growth perspective** is concerned primarily with employee performance and how it contributes to the growth of the business. Data on the amount spent on training and the number of new ideas generated by employees are typically used. See the example in Table 9.

Kaplan and Norton's balanced scorecard Measures business performance in terms of four perspectives: financial, customer, business process and learning and growth.

Elkington's triple bottom line Aims to encourage businesses to account for the social cost of their activities. The triple bottom line consists of financial, social and environmental costs.

Table 9 Kaplan and Norton's balanced scorecard as used by Sainsbury's in a strategy to target wealthier customers

	1. Main factors	2. What to measure	3. How to measure
Financial perspective	Revenue should at least stay stable as a result of the changes	Revenue per week compared with revenue in the same week last year	Use electronic till data adjusted by weather factors* for seasonal products *supplied by Met Office
	Gross profit margins rise as we move towards Waitrose pricing levels	Gross profit margins per department and for the store as a whole – compared with same week last year	Use electronic till data (at low/zero cost)
Customer perspective	Existing regular customers are happy	Change in £s spent this week per customer who came last week	Use Nectar (loyalty) card data (low/zero cost to us)
	New customers are attracted	Number of customers this week who have not shopped with us for at least 8 weeks	Market researchers sampling stores daily (cost: £20,000 per week)
Business process	Install more manned counters, such as fresh fish and/or cheese	£s per customer spent in total on fish/cheese with and without the manned counter	Measure pre/post change and measure among stores with and without counters (using till receipts, so low/zero cost)
	Check that wastage rates are not rising excessively now we are selling more fresh, unwrapped food	Average percentage of food sell-by date mark-down Average percentage of food thrown away	Measure pre/post change and measure among stores with and without counters (using till receipts, so low/zero cost)
Learning and growth	Staff need to develop a greater willingness to engage with and help customers	Customer feedback is needed on the degree and quality of staff engagement	Can use the same questionnaire process as above (sharing the £20,000 weekly cost)
	Encourage shop floor staff to put forward improvement ideas from customers	Measure the number of improvement suggestions per staff member	Store managers can record suggestions per staff member, rating quality on a 1–5 scale.

In order to implement the balanced scorecard, a company needs to set out a clear strategy and then consult with managers regarding:

- the main factors required for the strategy to succeed
- how best to measure each of these factors
- setting up methods to measure these factors.

The strength of this approach is that it provides a wider view of business performance, encourages the business to find measures that look to the present and future, and identifies factors that can be measured in terms of success.

However, it has been criticised due to the fact that employees may become too focused on simply achieving targets. Furthermore, if the targets set are unrealistic and/or imposed on employees, they will become demotivated. A final criticism is that drawing up the scorecard takes time and can be too rigid. Consequently, it could be inappropriate for businesses that operate in rapidly changing markets.

Elkington's triple bottom line

The triple bottom line is often known as 'profit, people and planet'. The idea is that it not only measures the financial performance of the business in terms of the amount of profit made but also attempts to quantify the social and environmental costs and benefits incurred by the business (see example in Table 10).

Table 10 An example of a 'triple bottom line'

	2016	2015	Notes on 2016
Profit for the year:	£4.5m	£3.5m	Successful trading year
Social gain/loss	(£0.4m)	(£0.6m)	More jobs provided this year
Environment	(£0.8m)	(£0.4m)	Our April '16 river pollution crisis
Triple bottom line	£3.3m	£2.5m	Overall, a successful year

The intention of this approach is to encourage businesses to be more socially responsible by accounting for all their activities. Unilever, which makes well-known brands such as Dove, Persil and Ben & Jerry's, has adopted some of the ideas of the triple bottom line through its 'Sustainable Living Plan'.

The strengths of this approach are that businesses become more accountable to all their stakeholders and they pay more attention to social and environmental factors. This would provide incentives for businesses to place more emphasis on issues such as improving working conditions for employees, treating suppliers fairly and reducing pollution.

However, in reality few companies have adopted this approach. A major problem is that it is often difficult to quantify social and environmental costs and benefits. Furthermore, for most public limited companies, the main priority is to keep shareholders happy rather than other stakeholders.

> **Knowledge check 28**
>
> What are social and environmental costs and benefits?

Exam tip

Kaplan and Norton's balanced scorecard model and Elkington's triple bottom line are both new concepts in the AQA specification. It is important that you develop a good understanding of these concepts, particularly when answering questions on how to measure business performance.

Summary

In this section you should be able to:
- Identify three measures of marketing performance.
- Identify three measures of human resource performance.
- Identify three measures of operations performance.
- Explain the importance of core competences for business success.
- Understand the difference between short- and long-term performance.
- Identify three features of a short-termist approach.
- Identify three features of a long-term approach.
- Explain Kaplan and Norton's balanced scorecard model.
- Explain Elkington's triple bottom line.
- Understand the strengths and weaknesses of Kaplan and Norton's balanced scorecard model and Elkington's triple bottom line.

Political and legal change

The impact on strategic and functional decision making

The **political and legal environment** affects all businesses. Many view political and legal change as a threat to their future success, but these changes can also create opportunities. In this section the effect of political and legal change on competition, the labour market and the environment will be examined.

Competition

Competition law is designed to encourage competition within markets to ensure that consumers have choice. If a market is dominated by one company, consumers suffer from higher prices and lack of choice. Furthermore, consumers may suffer from poor service and a lack of new products, due to the fact that the dominant business has little incentive to improve because of the lack of competition.

Competition law is designed to ensure that dominant businesses do not work together to restrict supply of products and charge artificially high prices. It is also intended to prevent a dominant business abusing its power by treating suppliers unfairly.

In the UK, the Competition and Markets Authority has the power to prevent certain mergers and takeovers. Specifically, if a merger or takeover would result in the business controlling more than 25% of a particular market, it would not be allowed. As a result, the business would have to pursue other strategies, such as entering into a joint venture with another business that would not involve a change in ownership, or attempting to increase its market share through internal growth.

The labour market

Employment law is intended to prevent the exploitation of employees by businesses. It covers areas such as:
- pay
- working conditions such as working hours plus health and safety
- equal opportunities such as preventing discrimination based upon sex or race
- the right to have trade union representation.

Political and legal environment Concerned with legislation passed by government that is usually a part of government policy. Businesses will be affected by both UK and European Union legislation.

Knowledge check 29

Identify three ways that increased competition forces a business to improve its performance.

A recent example of government legislation is the 'living wage'. This builds upon the minimum wage legislation that requires all employers to pay (at the time of writing) at least £6.50 per hour for all employees aged 21 and older. The 'living wage' is that amount considered necessary for an individual to have an acceptable standard of living.

Many UK businesses view the 'living wage' as a threat as it will increase their wage costs. This may force them to charge higher prices, which may make them uncompetitive compared with foreign competitors, whose wage costs are lower. As a result, many UK firms could move their operations to countries where wage costs are lower, such as China or India. Alternatively, they could become more capital intensive, by replacing workers with machines. However, some UK firms are happy to pay the 'living wage' as they believe it will provide them with many benefits.

Knowledge check 30

Think of three benefits to a business resulting from paying its employees the 'living wage'.

The environment

Environmental legislation is intended to minimise the negative impacts of business activity on the environment. It also aims to encourage businesses to be more accountable for any social costs that they create. Table 11 shows examples of such legislation.

Table 11 Examples of environmental protection legislation

Air pollution	Land pollution	Water pollution
Greenhouse gases and global warming	Waste disposal (Landfill Tax)	Recycling
Emission of 'particulate matter' from diesel cars	Planning permission for buildings	Waste treatment
Energy efficiency labelling	Building regulations	Water use
Energy use	Treatment of hazardous substances	Marine environment

In the UK the Environment Agency is responsible for the enforcement of environmental legislation. Businesses found to be breaking the law are subject to fines and possible closure if they do not improve their practices.

Many businesses initially considered environmental legislation as a threat due to the increased costs resulting from having to reduce the amount of pollution they created. Furthermore, businesses resented the extra time spent on the bureaucracy required to prove that they were complying with the legislation.

However, many businesses now view environmental legislation as an opportunity (see Figure 4). Through measures such as recycling, energy conservation and minimisation of waste, significant cost savings can be made. In addition, improving the environmental image of a business enhances its reputation and provides a USP. This may attract consumers and ethical investors. Marks and Spencer's 'Plan A' is a key strategy based upon the opportunities that may result from improved environmental performance. 'Plan A' involves achieving environmental objectives such as reducing waste, energy conservation and recycling.

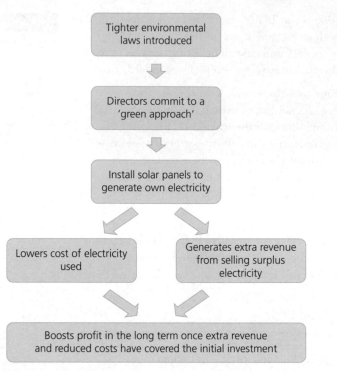

Figure 4 The benefits resulting from environmental legislation

Knowledge check 31

Identify one short-term cost and one long-term benefit resulting from environmental legislation.

Exam tip

When answering questions on the effect of legislation on business, always consider both the positive and the negative. It is important to consider the actual business in the question in terms of the type of product, amount of competition and type of customer.

The impact of UK and EU government policy

Government policy affects all businesses. As well as economic policy, governments will implement policies related to enterprise, the role of regulators, infrastructure, the environment and international trade.

Policies related to enterprise

The government has implemented policies to encourage and help people set up their own businesses. Examples include:

■ providing cheap finance through 'start-up loan' schemes
■ creating 'enterprise zones' to attract businesses to locate to regions suffering from high unemployment
■ providing advice and training.

The government has also set up schemes to help small and medium-sized businesses to expand through schemes such as:

■ the Business Finance Partnership, which provides cheap sources of finance
■ tax incentives such as reducing the taxes companies have to pay as a result of employing extra staff.

Policies related to the role of regulators

In industries that were once owned by the state, such as water, energy and the railways, the government appoints regulators who are responsible for ensuring that consumers are not exploited by dominant private sector firms. This is achieved by:

Government policy

Term that can be used to describe any course of action that intends to change a certain situation. Think of policies as a starting point for government to take a course of action that makes a real life change.

Knowledge check 32

Identify three reasons why the government wishes to encourage enterprise.

- price controls – dominant firms operating in a market are allowed to increase prices only by an amount set by the regulator, for instance gas and electricity prices
- regulating the product or service provided – certain minimum standards are set, which all firms in that industry must achieve, for example safety and/or punctuality standards for railway companies. Failure to meet these standards can result in financial penalties.

Policies related to infrastructure

Infrastructure is a very important factor that affects the competitiveness of a business. It has a direct effect upon productivity (see Figure 5). For example, an unreliable energy supply could result in power shortages. Consequently, factory output would be reduced. Congested roads may result in late deliveries, meaning that factory production could be threatened.

Figure 5 The business significance of infrastructure

Policies related to the environment

Government policy protects the environment in three ways:

- Green taxes – related to the amount of pollution created by a business. For example, businesses have to pay a 'landfill tax' for the disposal of physical waste.
- Subsidies – providing funds to businesses to encourage better environmental behaviour, for example subsidies to encourage greater use of renewable energy such as solar and wind power.
- Laws and regulations – covering a wide range of environmental practices such as the materials used, manufacturing processes and recycling.

Policies related to international trade

International trade is concerned with the import and export of goods and services between countries. Governments like to encourage the free trade of imports and exports between countries because it can raise living standards. This is because businesses and consumers can enjoy cheaper imported goods and services. Furthermore, it encourages specialisation by enabling businesses to focus on what they are best at.

Businesses also like international trade because it enables them to sell their products to foreign as well as domestic markets.

International trade can be restricted by **tariffs** and **quotas**. Governments will often impose tariffs on imported goods to protect their domestic industries.

Infrastructure Also known as social capital. It includes the road and rail network, access to utilities such as energy, water and broadband, education and medical facilities.

Knowledge check 33

Why is good infrastructure essential for a business that uses 'just in time' operations?

Knowledge check 34

Consider all the items that you own. How has international trade benefited you?

Tariffs Taxes that are imposed on imports. This results in them becoming more expensive.

Quotas Restrictions on the amount of a certain product that can be imported into a country.

Exam tip

The impact of government policy is often used as a topic for essay questions. This is because it covers a wide range of issues. When revising this topic always remember to consider both the opportunities and the threats that can result from government policy.

Knowledge check 35

Think of two reasons why a government would want to protect its own industries from foreign competition.

Summary

In this section you should be able to:
- Explain why government implements policies to encourage competition.
- Understand the main areas covered by employment legislation.
- Identify the costs and benefits to business resulting from environmental legislation.
- Explain why the government encourages enterprise.

- Understand how regulators have the power to protect consumers in certain markets.
- Define the term 'infrastructure'.
- Explain the importance of infrastructure for business.
- Understand how the government encourages businesses to protect the environment.
- Explain the benefits of international trade.
- Define the terms 'tariffs' and 'quotas'.

Economic change

The impact of changes in the UK and the global economic environment

Economic change refers to fluctuations in national and international 'macroeconomic' variables such as changes in exchange rates, inflation, unemployment and economic growth.

Gross domestic product (GDP)

GDP is the total value of all the goods and services produced by a country in a year. It is a measure of economic growth. Rising economic growth is good for both individuals and business. For individuals, it means that their standard of living is improving, enabling them to afford more goods and services. For business, rising economic growth provides more opportunities to sell more products and expand.

Economic growth is measured by the **business cycle**.

During a boom, GDP is rising rapidly, indicating high levels of economic growth. Booms are usually followed by periods of recession, defined as two successive quarters of negative GDP. Recessions can lead to a slump, which is a sustained period of negative GDP. The recovery phase of the business cycle is indicated by a return to a rise in GDP.

Changes in the business cycle affect businesses in different ways. This is often dependent upon the type of good or service that they sell. For example, firms that sell luxury goods such as sports cars and expensive jewellery tend to do well during periods of economic boom, but badly during a recession. Meanwhile, businesses that sell cheap goods, such as budget supermarkets, usually see an increase in sales during a recession but a fall during a boom.

Business cycle
Measures the regular pattern of ups and downs in GDP over time. It is characterised by four main phases: boom, recession, slump and recovery.

Table 12 illustrates the phases of the business cycle.

Table 12 The phases of the business cycle

	Boom	Recession	Slump	Recovery
Consumer and business confidence	Optimistic	Doubts emerging	Pessimistic	Gradually returning
Consumer spending	High. Low levels of saving. Spending supplemented by credit	Falling. Spending financed by credit starts to fall	Falling. Consumers save to pay off debts built up during the boom	Rising. Debts have now been paid off
Economic growth	Strongly positive	GDP begins to fall	GDP growth might now be strongly negative	Weak, but slowly improving
Unemployment	Close to zero	Low, but starting to rise	High	High, but starting to fall
Inflation	High, and possibly accelerating	Still positive, but falling. Firms now start to think twice about raising prices	Stable prices, or even some deflation (falling prices) is possible	Price stability
Number of firms failing	Low	Low, but rising	High	Falling
Business investment	Firms are optimistic about the future. Investment takes place for both replacement and expansion purposes	Falling. Expansion programmes may be postponed	Close to zero. Even replacement investment may have to be postponed to conserve cash	Slowly rising. Replacement investment projects previously postponed might now get the green light

Changes in the business cycle have an impact on business strategic and functional decision making. Businesses will have to change their objectives, and marketing, human resources, operations and finance will all have to change their functional strategies. For example, during a recession a car manufacturer may have to change its objective to survival. The marketing function may have to concentrate on promoting its cheaper models or offer lower prices. Operations may have to reduce capacity and cut its inventory levels. Human resources may have to make some workers redundant and/or reduce the number of working hours for each employee. Finally, finance may need to concentrate on cost cutting and ensuring that there is sufficient cash flow.

Exam tip

When answering questions on this topic, always consider the type of business in terms of the product or service that it sells. Remember that businesses are not all affected in the same way by changes in the business cycle.

Fiscal and monetary policy

The government attempts to influence the economy and how businesses operate through its economic policies. The two main policies it uses are **fiscal** and **monetary policy**.

The government collects taxes to pay for public services such as health, education, social security, the police and defence. The main forms of taxation are:

Knowledge check 36

Identify one business that would expect to see sales rise during an economic boom, one business that would expect its sales to fall, and another business that would not expect to see significant changes in its sales.

Fiscal policy Concerned with government tax and spending.

Monetary policy Involves the Bank of England setting interest rates, which influence the level of spending in the economy.

- income tax – this is based upon the amount of income an individual earns. The higher the income, the greater the rate of taxation
- national insurance – this is an additional tax paid by both business and employees
- value added tax (VAT) – this is a tax applied to most goods and services which businesses add to the price of their goods and services
- excise duties – these are taxes applied to specific products such as petrol, cigarettes and alcohol
- corporation tax – this is a tax on company profits.

Government spending has a direct effect upon both consumers and businesses. For example, if the government increases its spending on defence by building more fighter aircraft, the manufacturer will benefit from increased orders. In turn this will create extra employment as workers are recruited to build the aircraft. The additional income earned by the employees will be spent in the local economy, benefiting those businesses such as shops and restaurants.

Monetary policy is closely linked to the business cycle. During economic recession, the Bank of England will reduce interest rates. This makes it cheaper for consumers to borrow money for expensive items such as houses or cars. Businesses that sell these products will then benefit from increased demand and may take on additional workers. Due to increased sales, business confidence will rise. As a result, businesses are more likely to borrow to finance investment and expansion. This should result in economic recovery.

Exchange rates

Changes in the exchange rate can have a direct effect on the profitability of a business because the **exchange rate** affects the price of both imported and exported goods.

The impact of a high exchange rate

A high exchange rate means that the pound is worth more against other currencies. This means that UK goods are now more expensive for foreign customers. This could lead to a fall in demand as foreign customers may switch to cheaper alternatives.

However, a strong pound benefits UK firms that import foreign goods because they are now cheaper. This could lower their costs, enabling them to charge lower prices and so resulting in more demand. Alternatively, a business could keep the price the same but enjoy higher profit margins.

A low exchange rate has the opposite effect because the pound is worth less against foreign currencies. This results in UK exports being cheaper but imports being more expensive.

Exam tip

Remember that the success of a business is not affected solely by exchange rates. Although exchange rates affect both costs and prices, business success is also due to other factors such as customer service, product design and effective marketing.

Knowledge check 37

Think of another way that consumers may benefit from reduced interest rates and how this could benefit the economy.

Exchange rate
Measures the quantity of foreign currency that can be bought with one unit of another currency.

Exam tip

A useful acronym to use when revising exchange rates is SPICED: Strong Pound Imports Cheaper Exports Dearer.

Knowledge check 38

Why would UK tourist businesses prefer the exchange rate to be weak?

Inflation

Inflation measures the percentage annual rise in the level of prices. High rates of inflation are generally considered bad for business. This is because they increase a business's costs. For example, businesses may have to pay more for raw materials and energy. In order to retain profit margins, a business may increase its prices to cover these higher costs. This may result in uncompetitive prices and loss of sales to cheaper rivals.

Furthermore, rising inflation can create industrial relations problems. Employees will ask for higher wages to maintain living standards threatened by rising prices. Businesses may resist their demands because it will add to their costs and could make them uncompetitive. Consequently, this disagreement could lead to an industrial relations dispute.

Open trade versus protectionism

International trade creates both threats and opportunities for UK business. The opportunities include:

- access to international markets to increase sales and enable expansion
- the opportunity to source from cheaper overseas suppliers, resulting in lower production costs.

However, international trade can also create threats such as:

- increased competition in the UK market from foreign businesses
- greater vulnerability to changes in import and export prices resulting from changes in the exchange rate.

Protectionism is the opposite of open international trade. It is intended to make it more difficult for foreign businesses to sell their goods and services in domestic markets. The main forms of protectionism are tariffs and quotas. Protectionism is usually considered to be bad because it protects inefficient domestic businesses from more efficient foreign competitors and restricts consumer choice. Furthermore, countries can become involved in 'trade wars', resulting in a severe restriction in imports and exports between them. However, in certain circumstances protectionism can be justified in order to protect developing industries from more powerful foreign competitors or to protect domestic industries that have strategic importance.

Reasons for greater globalisation of business

Globalisation is concerned with the pressures leading to the world becoming one market. The growth of globalisation is due to a variety of reasons:

- a reduction in protectionism due to more countries joining the World Trade Organization (WTO), which has led to fewer tariffs and quotas
- multinational companies setting up factories and offices in different countries around the world
- improved transport and communication links enabling better distribution of goods and services as well as information.

Knowledge check 39

What could a business ask from its workforce in return for a pay rise, that could result in lower costs in the long term?

Knowledge check 40

At the time of writing, the UK government is under pressure to protect the UK steel industry from competition from cheap Chinese imported steel. Think of two reasons why the government should protect the UK steel industry.

Exam tip

Remember that economic change provides both opportunities and threats for business. When answering questions on this topic always consider the strategies a business could adopt to exploit potential opportunities and counter potential threats.

The importance of globalisation for business

Globalisation is important for business because it provides the following benefits:

- Businesses have the opportunity to learn from the best ideas from different countries, for example the introduction of Japanese lean production techniques to the UK car industry has resulted in greater productivity and quality.
- Direct foreign investment creates jobs and wealth.
- Greater foreign competition forces domestic businesses to improve in order to compete. As a result, consumers should benefit from more choice, better quality and competitive prices.
- The opportunity to sell their products overseas enables businesses to diversify. This spreads risk and means that they are no longer dependent upon one market.

However, globalisation also has its disadvantages, such as:

- Domestic businesses may be unable to compete with more powerful foreign rivals.
- Some multinationals have been criticised for exploiting the workforce in their factories, particularly in developing countries, through poor pay and working conditions.
- The majority of the wealth created by multinational companies goes back to their own countries. Consequently, the host country gains little benefit.

The importance of emerging economies for business

Emerging economies are becoming increasingly important for business. Traditionally businesses would take advantage of the lower production costs in emerging economies, enabling them to source their products at a cheaper price. This was particularly true in industries such as clothing and electronics.

More recently, due to the benefits of globalisation, a growing 'middle class' of consumers in emerging economies has developed. These consumers are interested in and have the income to purchase Western products. Combined with the fact that many emerging economies also have large populations, there now exists a huge market which is very attractive for Western companies (Table 13).

> **Knowledge check 41**
>
> Identify three reasons why Jaguar Land Rover (JLR) has benefited from manufacturing and selling its cars in China.

Emerging economy One that has the potential to grow in terms of productive capacity, market opportunities and competitive advantage.

Table 13 Economic performance of selected emerging economies

	GDP at PPP 2013	Average annual growth in GDP per head 1970–90	Average annual growth in GDP per head 1990–2012	Percentage of population below $1.25 a day 2007–11
Bangladesh	$2,100	0.5	3.7	43
Cambodia	$2,600	0.0	6.0	19
China	$9,800	6.6	9.3	12
India	$4,000	2.0	5.0	33
Nicaragua	$4,500	-3.7	2.0	12
Nigeria	$2,800	-1.3	2.1	54

Source: CIA Factbook 2015 and Unicef statistics 2015

This is particularly true for China, which has rapidly become the world's biggest exporter, but also, after the USA, the world's second biggest importer (see Figure 6).

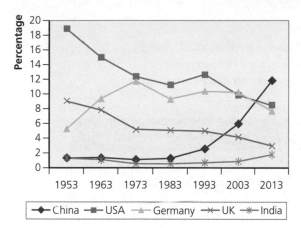

Figure 6 World share of exports of goods, 1953–2013

Source: World Trade Organization, January 2015

Knowledge check 42

Identify three reasons why China is now a leading world exporter and importer.

Exam tip

Questions on globalisation and emerging economies often focus on the opportunities offered. Remember that in order to exploit these opportunities, businesses need to have a detailed strategy based upon careful research, which understands the cultural differences that exist in emerging economies.

Summary

In this section you should be able to:
- Understand the four phases of the business cycle.
- Explain how different businesses are affected by the changes in the business cycle.
- Define 'fiscal' and 'monetary' policy.
- Explain how government spending can affect business performance.
- Understand the significance of interest rates for both consumers and business.

- Remember what the acronym SPICED stands for.
- Explain why high inflation is usually bad for business.
- Define the term 'globalisation'.
- Understand the reasons why globalisation is important for business.
- Explain two reasons why emerging economies are important for some UK businesses.

Social and technological opportunities and threats

The impact on strategic and functional decision making

Social change is another key component of the external environment that businesses need to be aware of. It can provide both opportunities and threats, which require businesses to implement strategies in response to them. In this section, three examples of social change will be considered:

- urbanisation and migration
- changes in consumer lifestyle and buying behaviour
- the growth of online businesses.

Social change Refers to the fluidity of human behaviour and actions that affect demography and lifestyle.

Urbanisation and migration

Urbanisation occurs when more of the population move from rural areas to live in towns and cities (Table 14). It usually occurs as a result of economic growth. This is because the jobs created by business tend to be concentrated in urban areas.

Table 14 Percentage of the population living in urban areas

Country	Percentage of population living in urban areas 2014	Percentage of population living in urban areas 2000
UK	82	79
USA	81	79
China	54	36
Brazil	85	81
India	32	28
Malawi	16	15

Source: World Bank

Urbanisation provides opportunities for business because it means that there are large numbers of people concentrated in towns and cities. This represents an attractive target market.

Migration occurs when people move from one country to another. Most businesses consider migration to be important for their future success. This is because:

- it enables them to recruit workers with specialist skills that may not exist in sufficient quantity domestically
- it increases the choice of available workers
- it can keep wage costs lower as migrant workers are often prepared to accept the 'living wage' while some UK workers may not be
- certain sectors such as agriculture, hotels and restaurants are heavily dependent upon migrant workers because many UK workers do not want to work in these sectors
- large numbers of migrant workers can represent attractive niche markets, for example many supermarkets now have food sections aimed specifically at certain migrant groups.

> **Knowledge check 43**
>
> Identify two social costs that may arise as a result of increased urbanisation and migration.

Changes in consumer lifestyle and buying behaviour

Most people now have busier lives and as a consequence their time is often at a premium. Consequently, consumers increasingly value convenience when purchasing goods and services. Businesses have had to respond to this in a variety of ways, for example:

- the growth in convenience foods such as 'ready meals'
- home delivery of products
- the rise in supermarket convenience stores, particularly in large towns and cities.

Technology has also had a major effect upon buying behaviour. The internet has provided consumers with more information about products and services. Consequently, they are now better informed, meaning that businesses need to be more competitive. Also consumer tastes can now change more rapidly and firms have to be more responsive. For example, through social media consumers are constantly aware of changes in fashion and are keen to wear the latest trends. This has led to the growth of 'fast fashion' which has been exploited successfully by companies such as Zara and H&M.

The growth of online businesses

In early 2015, online sales in the UK were £104 billion, representing nearly 25% of total retail sales (see Figure 7). The rapid growth in online sales is due to the increased use of technology and the importance that consumers attach to convenience when purchasing products.

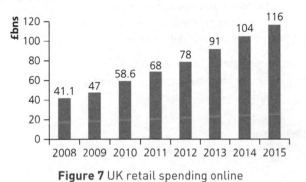

Figure 7 UK retail spending online

Online businesses have succeeded for the following reasons:

- increased usage of the internet, particularly through smartphones and tablet computers
- convenience offered by direct delivery or 'click and collect' services
- the growth of social media and apps, which provide consumers with more information as well as greater convenience when purchasing goods and services.

Online business has created numerous opportunities which have been successfully exploited by companies such as Amazon and ASOS. However, many retail stores have suffered as they failed to respond quickly enough to consumers' growing preference for buying online.

The pressures for socially responsible behaviour

An important element of the social environment is the concept of **corporate social responsibility (CSR)**.

CSR includes the following actions:

- treating customers fairly and honestly
- protecting the environment
- providing employees with good pay and conditions
- paying the correct amount of taxation
- not being involved in anti-competitive practices
- providing accurate financial information.

Reasons for CSR

Being seen as a socially responsible business can create marketing benefits, as it can differentiate a business from its rivals. Many consumers are keen to buy products from businesses that are morally correct, and are often prepared to pay higher prices.

Knowledge check 44

Think of three reasons why a retail store would struggle to compete with an online business such as Amazon or ASOS.

Exam tip

Remember that when answering questions on social change, you should always consider the importance of business strategy in determining how the business should respond. The strategy needs to consider how each functional area should adapt.

Corporate social responsibility (CSR) A form of self-regulation by which companies exceed minimum legal requirements in an attempt to be good social citizens.

Being socially responsible can also create a good reputation for the business as an employer. This can enable the business to attract good quality staff as well as retain a motivated workforce. The business will then benefit from lower labour turnover, better quality and higher productivity.

Reasons against CSR

Some shareholders may oppose a business becoming more socially responsible as it could have a negative effect upon profitability. For example, a socially responsible business may choose 'fairtrade' suppliers rather than the cheapest one available. Furthermore, certain business opportunities may be rejected despite the fact that they are potentially profitable, because they could be considered morally incorrect, for example selling products to governments that have a bad human rights record.

An additional criticism is that some businesses simply view CSR as a public relations tool in order to gain good publicity but fail to implement the actions required from a socially responsible business (see Figure 8).

Figure 8 Is CSR authentic or cosmetic?

The stakeholder versus the shareholder concept

The **stakeholder** concept is when the managers of a business consider it is important to focus on the needs of all stakeholders when making major decisions. For example, if a business decides to relocate, the effect upon the employees and the local community would be a major factor to consider.

This approach has been criticised because it can create conflicts between stakeholder groups. For example, employees would have the objective of better pay and conditions but this might conflict with the objectives of shareholders, who would fear that these additional costs could damage profitability.

The shareholder concept is based upon the idea that all business decisions should be based solely upon the interests of shareholders. This is because the shareholders own the business and appoint managers to run the business in their best interests. This

---

Knowledge check 45

Think of three businesses that you consider to be socially responsible.

Stakeholder An individual or group that has an effect on or is affected by the activities of an organisation. Stakeholders include shareholders, employees, customers and suppliers.

usually means maximising shareholder value through generating high profits in order to create good dividends and a rising share price.

Carroll's social responsibility pyramid

Professor Archie Carroll devised a pyramid that illustrates the different responsibilities, in order of priority, to be considered in order to be socially responsible (see Figure 9).

Figure 9 Carroll's social responsibility pyramid

Source: Carroll (1996)

The first priority is economic responsibilities. This is to ensure that the business is financially viable by providing sustainable profits.

The second priority is legal responsibilities, i.e. that the business is meeting all legal requirements.

This is followed by ethical responsibilities. This means that the business behaves in a morally correct manner and goes beyond the minimum legal requirements.

Finally, the business should meet its philanthropic responsibilities by contributing to society through actions such as making charitable donations and supporting local community projects.

Technological change

Technological change in both new products and manufacturing processes is occurring at a rapid rate.

Technological change provides both opportunities and threats for business. The opportunities include:

- quicker development of new products through applications such as computer aided design (CAD) and computer aided manufacture (CAM)
- development of new products can create new markets, for example digital streaming of music and film to 'SMART' televisions
- improved manufacturing processes can lead to better quality and higher productivity.

Knowledge check 46

What is a potential problem for a business if it considers just the interests of its shareholders rather than those of other stakeholders?

Exam tip

Carroll's social responsibility pyramid is a new concept on the AQA specification. When answering questions on CSR, it is a useful concept to use.

Technological change
The adaptation of new applications of practical or mechanical sciences to industry and commerce.

The threats include:

- shorter product life cycles due to new products constantly entering the market, for example smartphones
- the high cost of investment in new technology
- knowing the best time to invest in new technology – failing to respond quickly enough could result in the business being left behind by its rivals.

Technological change affects all the functional areas of a business (Table 15). For example, sophisticated accounting software can assist the finance department with activities such as budgeting. However, the human resource department may face challenges such as the additional training required to enable employees to use the new technology.

Table 15 The impact of technological change on different functional areas

	Internal technological change	External technological change
Marketing	Technological change can boost a firm's understanding of consumer behaviour with far greater computing power to analyse marketing data. New product development is a critical function for firms competing in technology-driven markets.	New media have become available to widen the promotional options available, whilst the internet has brought new distribution channels. Product developments that use technology can have a huge effect on markets – creating new ones or destroying long-standing markets for obsolete products such as non-digital cameras.
Finance	As computer software develops, financial information can be more easily recorded, processed and perhaps most powerfully shared within the business on an almost immediate basis. Finance departments must be heavily involved in any decision to purchase new technology given the size of investment that is usually involved.	The internet has made financial information much more easily available – perhaps heightening one of the drawbacks of limited company status. However, the ability for public limited companies to share financial reporting data with shareholders and potential investors may be a benefit.
Human resources	Firms adopting new technology may well find that staff need to be made redundant as technology takes over jobs previously filled by people. Not only is this likely to be in traditional contexts, where machines take over repetitive manual production tasks, but computers may now be able to assess information, such as X-rays to identify basic medical issues, taking over the role of medical staff. Other significant implications are the need to provide training for staff who are expected to use new technology and/or the need to recruit staff skilled in the use of new technology.	Technology can lead to unemployment, which of course causes problems for government and society. Technological change has also led to an increase in the amount of teleworking that can happen, with staff working from home.
Operations	Technology can have a revolutionary effect on operations management, not only in the way products are manufactured but also in the way that services are delivered. The drive to boost productivity is the underpinning factor behind the adoption of new technology – a constant desire to lower costs through finding technological solutions to the problem of how to lower unit costs.	Technological development in operations departments have had knock on effects on suppliers – with a greater ability to share information with suppliers, the chance to work in a genuine long-term partnership with customers has made many firms value the role played by their suppliers even more.

The strategic response by a business to technological change is dependent upon the technology itself, the business's resources and the management's attitude to change. A key issue when implementing new technology is how well the business overcomes the resistance to change from its employees, who will often feel threatened. The business must also consider whether the benefits resulting from investing in new technology outweigh the initial cost.

Knowledge check 47

Identify three uses of technology for the marketing function of a fashion clothing company.

Exam tip

Questions on technological change will often require you to assess its appropriateness for the actual business featured. Remember to consider this in relation to factors such as the size and resources of the business, the product it makes and its target market.

Summary

In this section you should be able to:
- Explain the reasons for urbanisation.
- Understand the benefits to business of migration.
- Explain why online business is growing rapidly.
- Define corporate social responsibility.
- Explain the reasons for and against a business becoming more socially responsible.
- Understand Carroll's social responsibility pyramid.
- Define technological change.
- Explain the opportunities and threats to business resulting from technological change.
- Understand how technological change impacts the functional areas of a business.
- Explain the factors that determine the strategy a business should consider when devising a strategy for technological change.

The competitive environment

The impact of Porter's five forces

Porter's five forces, shown in Figure 10, is a model that shows the main pressures on a business that determine its ability to compete and succeed.

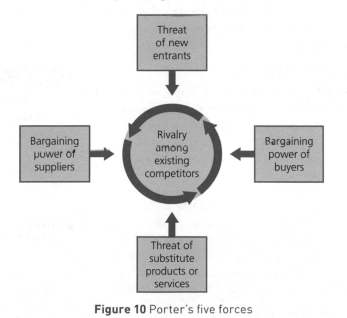

Figure 10 Porter's five forces

Source: 'The five competitive forces that shape strategy' by Michael E. Porter, *Harvard Business Review*, January 2008

It consists of the following.

1 Rivalry among existing competitors

Markets can be classified according to the degree of competition that exists. A monopoly is a market dominated by one business. According to the Competition and Markets Authority, a monopoly is when a business has a market share greater than 25%. An oligopoly is when a market is dominated by a few large companies. Finally, a competitive market consists of many small businesses, none of which has a dominant market share.

According to Porter, the amount of competition determines how the business should respond. For example, in an oligopoly, firms tend to adopt non-price competition strategies, whereas in a competitive market being able to offer lower prices is a key source of competitive advantage.

2 Threat of new entrants

As well as existing rivals, businesses must consider the potential threat of new entrants to their market. This is particularly the case in markets that are growing and when existing businesses are all making high profits. The threat of new entrants is determined by the **barriers to entry**. Businesses that operate in markets that have relatively few barriers to entry need to be constantly aware of the threat of new entrants and the need to devise strategies to combat them.

3 Changes in the buying power of customers

The power of customers is linked to how important they are to the business. If a business is dependent upon one large customer for a significant amount of its sales, it is in a vulnerable position as this customer could demand large price discounts. Conversely, if the business has many customers, it is in a stronger position. However, due to the greater availability of information through the internet, individual customers are better informed and more prepared to switch to more competitive rivals. This means that businesses now have to work a lot harder to retain all of their customers.

4 Changes in the selling power of suppliers

The power of suppliers is related to their ability to dictate the price they can charge to the business. If there is one dominant supplier, the business may have no alternative but to obtain its raw materials from it. Consequently, it may have to pay higher prices which could increase its costs and lower profit margins. Alternatively, if a business has a choice of several suppliers, it is in a more powerful position and will be able to negotiate lower prices.

5 Threat of substitutes

Substitutes represent alternative goods or services that consumers can choose compared with what the business offers. A good example is the car market. Rather than purchasing petrol-driven cars as a means of transport, alternatively consumers could buy an electric car. In addition, consumers may prefer to travel by bus or rail rather than drive. Technological change is often an important source of substitute products.

Porter's five forces model is a valuable tool for firms in helping them devise future strategic and functional decisions. By constantly assessing its competitive environment, a business can devise strategies to exploit opportunities and counter

Barriers to entry The factors that determine the accessibility of a market for potential new entrants. These include the cost required to set up a new business, the degree of brand loyalty to existing firms and any patents owned by existing firms.

Knowledge check 48

Would you consider the barriers to entry of the computer games market to be low or high? Explain two reasons why.

Knowledge check 49

Think of three substitute products available to consumers when purchasing a holiday, compared with buying from a travel agent.

threats. For example, if a business is faced with a new competitor or substitute, it may decide to remove the potential threat by taking over that rival. Alternatively, if its existing market is becoming increasingly competitive, the business may decide to diversify and enter another market.

Exam tip

Porter's five forces is a useful model to refer to when answering questions on business strategy. Examiners are usually impressed when students use relevant theory to support their arguments and may award high marks for analysis.

Summary

In this section you should be able to:
- Draw a diagram of Porter's five forces.
- Explain how each of the five forces can affect a business's competitive position.
- Recognise the relative importance of each of the five forces to the success of a particular business.

- Understand that due to changes in the competitive environment, the relative importance of each of the five forces can change.
- Explain how Porter's five forces are used by a business for making strategic and functional decisions.

Investment appraisal

Financial methods of assessing an investment

In order to make investment decisions using quantitative information, a business will use **investment appraisal** methods (Table 16).

Table 16 The data required to take effective decisions using investment appraisal

Decisions requiring investment appraisal	Information needed to make the decision
Should we launch new product A or B?	Sales forecasts, pricing decisions, and data on fixed, variable and start-up costs
Should we make a takeover bid for L'Oreal?	Forecast of future cash flows into and out of L'Oreal; compare the results with the purchase price
Shall we expand capacity by running a night shift?	Forecast of the extra costs compared with extra revenues

The three investment appraisal methods used are:
- payback period
- average rate of return
- net present value.

Payback period

This method calculates how long it will take to recover the initial cost of the investment.

Investment appraisal
Using forecasted cash flows to estimate the value of an investment decision based on quantitative criteria.

Content Guidance

A business invests £60,000 in a machine that will cost £10,000 per year to run but will generate £30,000 in revenue per year. The machine is expected to last 5 years (Table 17).

Table 17 Cash-flow table for the machine

	Cash in	Cash out	Net cash flow	Cumulative cash total
NOW*		£60,000	(£60,000)	(£60,000)
Year 1	£30,000	£10,000	£20,000	(£40,000)
Year 2	£30,000	£10,000	£20,000	(£20,000)
Year 3	£30,000	£10,000	£20,000	
Year 4	£30,000	£10,000	£20,000	£20,000
Year 5	£30,000	£10,000	£20,000	£40,000

In this example the initial £60,000 is recovered in exactly 3 years because the machine generates £20,000 of cash each year. In some cases an investment will not generate the same amount of cash each year. This can result in payback occurring between years. For example, see Table 18.

Table 18 Finding the payback period

	Cash in	Cash out	Net cash flow	Cumulative cash total
NOW		£40,000	(£40,000)	(£40,000)
Year 1	£20,000	£5,000	£15,000	(£25,000)
Year 2	£30,000	£10,000	£20,000	(£5,000)
Year 3	£36,000	£24,000	£12,000	£7,000

In this case payback occurs between years 2 and 3. To calculate the exact payback period, the following formula is used:

$$\frac{\text{outlay outstanding}}{\text{monthly cash in year of payback}}$$

For example:

$$\frac{£5,000}{£12,000} \times 12 = 5 \text{ months}$$

Payback is 2 years and 5 months.

Payback is particularly useful for projects where time is critical, for example in fast-changing markets such as fashion or technology. In these situations it is important that the cost of the investment is recovered quickly because there is less time available for generating profits. However, a criticism of payback is that longer investment projects in terms of payback may be rejected, despite the fact that in the long run they may be more profitable (Table 19).

Table 19 The advantages and disadvantages of payback

Advantages of payback	Disadvantages of payback
Easy to calculate and understand	Provides no insight into profitability
May be more accurate than other measures, because it ignores longer-term forecasts (the ones beyond the payback period)	Ignores what happens after the payback period
Takes into account the timing of cash flows	May encourage a short-termist attitude
Especially important for a business with weak cash flow; it may be willing to invest only in projects with a quick payback	Is not very useful on its own (because it ignores profit), therefore is used together with ARR or NPV (see below)

Average rate of return (ARR)

This method compares the average annual profit generated by an investment as a percentage of the initial cost. It is calculated using the formula:

$$\frac{\text{average annual return}}{\text{initial cost}} \times 100$$

The calculation of ARR consists of three steps:

1 Calculate the total return of the investment (sum of net cash flows − initial cost).

2 Divide the total return by the number of years of the investment to calculate the annual return.

3 Then apply the formula.

Worked example

BJ Carpets invests £20,000 in a new machine which is expected to last 4 years (Table 20).

Table 20 Figures for BJ Carpets

Year	Net cash flow	Cumulative cash flow
0	(£20,000)	(£20,000)
1	£5,000	(£15,000)
2	£11,000	(£4,000)
3	£10,000	£6,000
4	£10,000	£16,000

Step 1   Total return = £36,000 − £20,000 = £16,000

Step 2   Annual return = £16,000/4 = £4,000

Step 3   ARR = $\dfrac{£4,000}{£20,000} \times 100 = 20\%$

Average rate of return is useful because it focuses on profitability. The investment project that is the most profitable will be the one chosen. However, it does not take into account the timing of the returns, which could be important in fast-changing markets (Table 21).

Table 21 The advantages and disadvantages of average rate of return

Advantages of average rate of return	Disadvantages of average rate of return
Uses all the cash flows over the project's life...	... but, because later years are included, the results will not prove as accurate as payback
Focuses upon profitability	Ignores the timing of the cash flows
Easy to compare percentage returns on different investments, to help make a decision	Ignores the time value (opportunity cost) of the money invested

Net present value (NPV)

This method has the advantage of considering both timing and profitability. It is based upon the notion of discounted cash flows. These recognise the fact that the value of money falls over time. Businesses need to calculate the value of money received in the future in today's terms. These are known as present values. To calculate present values a discount factor is used based upon the length of time the investment will last and the current rate of interest. Present values are calculated by multiplying the net return by the discount factor. NPV is then calculated by subtracting the initial cost from the sum of the present values.

Exam tip

In the exam you will be given the discount factor to use. It is not important that you understand why that particular discount factor was chosen.

Worked example

A business is considering two alternative investment projects, Project Z and Project Y. Both cost £250,000. A 10% discount factor has been chosen.

Table 22 Project Z versus Project Y

	Project Z			Project Y		
Year	Cash flow	Discount factor	Present value (£s)	Cash flow	Discount factor	Present value (£s)
0	(£250,000)	1.00	(£250,000)	(£250,000)	1.00	(£250,000)
1	£50,000	0.91	£45,500	£200,000	0.91	£182,000
2	£100,000	0.83	£83,000	£100,000	0.83	£83,000
3	£200,000	0.75	£150,000	£50,000	0.75	£37,500
		NPV =	+£28,500		NPV =	+£52,500

The project with the greatest NPV is the one chosen. In this example it would be Project Y.

The benefit of NPV is that as well as considering both timing and profitability, the figures used are more accurate. However, it is a more complex calculation and the accuracy of figures is dependent upon the most realistic discount factor being chosen (Table 23).

Knowledge check 50

Write down the formulae for calculating payback, ARR and NPV.

Table 23 The advantages and disadvantages of NPV

Advantages of NPV	Disadvantages of NPV
Takes the opportunity cost of money into account	Complex to calculate and communicate
A single measure that takes the amount and timing of cash flows into account	The meaning of the result is often misunderstood
Can consider different scenarios	Only comparable between projects if the initial investment is the same

When performing investment appraisal calculations, always start with a table that shows the net return for each year. Remember to write down all your calculations and work methodically from one stage to the next.

Factors influencing investment decisions

As well as quantitative information, investment decisions must be based upon qualitative factors. These may include the following:

- Company objectives – the chosen investment must contribute to the achievement of future objectives.
- The financial position of the business – the effect upon gearing if the money required for the investment is borrowed, or possible cash flow issues, particularly for projects that have longer payback periods.
- Source of the data – are the data from an independent, reliable source?
- Effect upon staff – could the proposed investment create redundancies and/or require additional staff training?

Other factors that need to be considered are **investment criteria** and **risk and uncertainty**.

When answering questions on this topic, remember to consider both quantitative and qualitative factors. You may be given information in the case study about the business in question – always use this as an important source of qualitative information when considering whether a proposed investment should go ahead.

The value of sensitivity analysis

Sensitivity analysis is used for financial techniques such as:

- cash-flow forecasting
- breakeven analysis
- investment appraisal
- profit and contribution calculations.

It enables managers to assess the level of risk associated with a business decision and to assess which variables have the greatest potential impact (Table 24).

Investment criteria
The minimum financial targets set by the directors which the proposed investment must achieve, e.g. an ARR of at least 15%.

Risk and uncertainty
The recognition that all future returns are based upon predictions. The greater the future time span of the investment, the greater the risk and uncertainty. It is important for businesses to recognise that future figures could be inaccurate.

Think of three reasons why the figures for future returns for an investment project could be inaccurate.

Sensitivity analysis
Concerned with 'what if' scenarios. This means changing the variables in different financial forecasting models in order to assess the possible consequences for a business.

Table 24 Sensitivity analysis scenarios

	Type of calculation				
	Payback	**ARR**	**NPV**	**Cash-flow forecast**	**Breakeven**
Variables that can be adjusted	Cash in Cash out Initial investment	Cash in Cash out Initial investment Estimated duration of project	Cash in Cash out Initial investment Estimated duration of project Discount rate used	Selling price Expected sales Credit period offered Cash outflows Credit period received	Selling price Variable cost per unit Fixed costs

Sensitivity analysis helps managers in both planning and monitoring. Asking 'what if' questions is important before making business decisions because it raises awareness of the level of uncertainty and ensures that managers are aware of the possible negative consequences.

Knowledge check 52

Why should a business conduct sensitivity analysis regarding a change in interest rates?

Summary

In this section you should be able to:
- Remember how to calculate payback.
- Understand the advantages and disadvantages of payback.
- Remember how to calculate ARR.
- Understand the advantages and disadvantages of ARR.
- Remember how to calculate NPV.
- Understand the advantages and disadvantages of NPV.
- Identify three qualitative factors that affect an investment decision.
- Explain why risk and uncertainty for investment decisions increase over time.
- Define 'sensitivity analysis'.

Explain why sensitivity analysis is important for decision making.

■Choosing strategic direction

Which markets to compete in and what products to offer

Influencing factors

Strategic decisions are concerned with the long-term future of the business. They form the plan required to achieve the business's objectives. Strategic decisions require detailed research and consideration by the senior managers of the business.

Strategy should be:
- based upon the strengths of the business
- realistic and achievable
- based upon consideration of market potential and the business's resources
- based upon consideration of economic and social factors
- company specific, related to the individual circumstances of the business.

The reasons and value of different options for strategic direction

A useful technique for a business to use when considering its strategic direction is **Ansoff's matrix**.

The risks involved in strategic decisions are related to the firm's level of knowledge regarding its market, competitors and customers, both now and in the future. According to Ansoff, the risks become greater the further a business moves away from

Ansoff's matrix
Constructed to enable a business to consider the risks involved in strategic decisions.

a core strategy of focusing its existing products on its existing customers. However, the greater the risks, the greater the potential reward (see Figure 11).

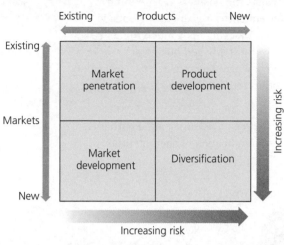

Figure 11 Ansoff's matrix and risk

Market penetration

This strategy is about increasing market share by concentrating on existing products within the existing market. This strategy has the least risk because the business is focusing on what it knows best. Examples of market penetration include:

- taking customers from competitors in the same market through aggressive marketing campaigns
- persuading existing customers to buy more of the product by suggesting additional ways to increase their usage.

Market development

This strategy is concerned with finding new markets for existing products. This is riskier because the business is attempting to sell its products to a target market that is different from its existing one. It is important that market research is carried out in order to gain good understanding of the business's new target customer's needs. Examples of market development include:

- repositioning the product by aiming it at a different market segment, e.g. Lucozade sports drinks
- targeting overseas markets, e.g. Jaguar Land Rover expanding into emerging economies such as China and India.

Product development

This strategy involves launching new products into an existing market. This is riskier because new products have a high rate of failure. It is estimated that only one out of every seven new products succeeds. The danger of this strategy for a business is that it will incur high costs of research and development, market research and promotion, which will not be recovered if the product fails. However, a business that successfully launches a new product enjoys the benefits of 'first mover advantage'. Examples of product development include:

- updating an existing product, e.g. by renaming it or changing the packaging
- developing a new, different product.

Knowledge check 53

What market penetration strategies are used by media companies such as Sky, Virgin Media and BT?

Knowledge check 54

Think of a company that has updated an existing product and another that has launched a totally new product.

Diversification

This is considered to be the riskiest strategy because the business is launching a new product that is aimed at a new market. Consequently, it is operating outside its range of knowledge and experience. This means that there is a much higher risk of failure. Although there are many examples of well-established businesses whose attempt at diversification was unsuccessful, there are also businesses that have gained enormous rewards. For example, the leading clothes retailer Primark is a subsidiary of Associated British Foods.

Ansoff's matrix enables businesses to assess the degree of risk associated with a particular strategic direction, but it also provides an indication of the potential rewards (see Figure 12).

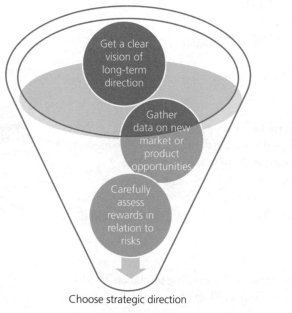

Figure 12 Implementing Ansoff's matrix

Summary

In this section you should be able to:
- Define 'business strategy'.
- Understand the key elements of an effective strategy.
- Draw a diagram of Ansoff's matrix.
- Explain market penetration.
- Explain market development.
- Explain product development.
- Explain diversification.
- Understand business examples of each of Ansoff's strategies.
- Explain the potential risks and rewards of each of Ansoff's strategies.

Strategic positioning: choosing how to compete

Benefits and price

When choosing how to compete, a business must consider the best way to gain a **competitive advantage**.

Strategic positioning

Businesses need to decide how they are going to position themselves in their particular market. Common factors that determine how a business competes include the price charged for its products as well as the benefits they provide for its customers. Two commonly used business models for strategic positioning are **Porter's generic strategies** and **Bowman's strategic clock**.

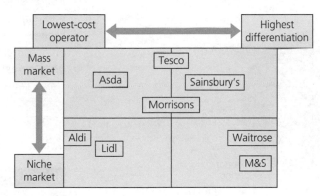

Figure 13 Porter's generic strategies for the UK supermarket sector

Porter considered that a business must decide which one of two options it should choose when adopting its strategic position (see Figure 13). These should be either low cost or differentiation. Businesses that aim to do both face the problem of being 'stuck in the middle'. This may result in customers being confused by what the business stands for and consequently competitiveness may suffer.

Porter's low-cost strategy is based upon the business aiming to be the lowest-cost operator in its market. The focus is upon cost minimisation achieved through high levels of efficiency. Being the lowest-cost operator is a source of competitive advantage because it enables the business to charge lower prices than its rivals. Alternatively, the business can charge the same price as its competitors but enjoy higher profit margins.

Porter's differentiation strategy is based upon the concept of added value. The business aims to provide a good or service that consumers consider to be superior to its rivals. Consequently, consumers are prepared to pay a premium price. Differentiation strategy is often dependent upon the business achieving a strong brand image, resulting in brand loyalty and customers who are buying the brand and are not concerned about the price.

Knowledge check 56

Name one car manufacturer and one technology business that successfully adopts a differentiation strategy.

Competitive advantage When a business is able to differentiate itself from its rivals and increase its market share.

Porter's generic strategies A matrix suggesting that all markets operate in the same way. They can be segmented in two ways: mass versus niche markets and lowest cost versus differentiation strategies.

Bowman's strategic clock A statement of eight different strategic positions that a business could adopt based upon the variables of price and customer value.

Knowledge check 55

Name one business in the clothing market and one business in the airline market that successfully adopts a low-cost strategy.

Porter's focused low-cost strategy is adopted by businesses in niche markets. Consequently, it tends to be used by small or medium-sized businesses. For example, in the grocery sector, a corner shop may consistently aim to be cheaper than its rivals for certain products such as bread and milk.

Porter's focused differentiation strategy is used in niche markets. It is often found in luxury markets for products such as expensive clothing and jewellery. To be successful this strategy needs to be based upon an exclusive image, enabling the business to charge extremely high prices.

For each strategy the key to long-term success for a business is to maintain the source of its competitive advantage. Businesses that adopt a low-cost strategy must consistently be able to operate more efficiently than their rivals, while a differentiation strategy is reliant upon the business maintaining its USP.

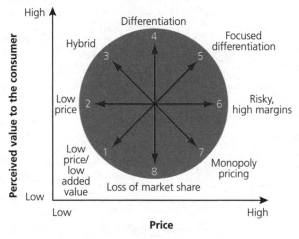

Figure 14 Bowman's strategic clock

Source: from *Competitive and Corporate Strategy* by
Cliff Bowman and David Faulkner, 1997

According to Bowman, the best strategies a business should adopt are those that customers perceive have the highest value. For example, the strategies of 'hybrid', 'differentiation' and 'focused differentiation' have the highest perceived customer value according to Bowman's strategic clock (see Figure 14).

Influences on the choice of a positioning strategy

The choice of the positioning strategy taken up by a business is dependent upon the consideration of the following factors:

■ The strengths and weaknesses of the business – this is often based upon the background and tradition of the business. For example, what are the skills and experience of the senior managers based on?
■ The positioning of competitors within the same market – for example, if rival businesses have adopted a low-cost approach, there may be a gap in the market for the business to adopt a differentiation strategy.
■ The skills of the workforce – for example, a business with a highly skilled, creative workforce is more likely to adopt a differentiation strategy.

- How competitive is the market – if a business is competing against a dominant rival, it may decide to position itself in a different market where there is a greater chance of success.

The value of different strategic positioning strategies

Michael Porter's generic strategies are widely considered to be a valuable business model. The main reason for this is that the model has a clear message: simply, that to be successful a business must either focus on 'low cost' or 'differentiation'. Businesses that try to do both will confuse customers and risk being 'stuck in the middle'.

A criticism of Porter is that this model tends to work best in settled, slow-moving markets, but in fast-changing markets businesses that fail to adapt their strategic position may get left behind. This is because in these markets it is more difficult to sustain competitive advantage due to changing consumer tastes and threats from new rivals. For example, in China, Apple's differentiation strategy for its iPhone has been challenged by domestic rivals such as Huawei, whose smartphones have gained in popularity among Chinese consumers.

The benefits of having a competitive advantage

Competitive advantage provides many benefits for a business (see Figure 15), including:

- Increased profits – these can be reinvested into new equipment, product development and staff training, which can lead to improved performance as well as enabling the business to sustain its competitive advantage.
- Increased sales and market share – the business can become more dominant in its market and fund expansion through increased sales revenue.
- Higher capacity utilisation – increased sales result in increased output to meet the demand. Higher capacity utilisation means that the business is operating more efficiently as fixed costs are spread over more units of production. As a result, unit (average) costs fall, enabling the business to reduce its prices or retain its prices but benefit from higher profit margins.
- Economies of scale – as the business becomes bigger it benefits from economies of scale, resulting in lower unit costs.

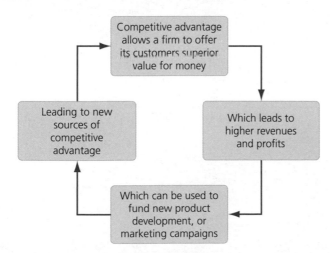

Figure 15 How competitive advantage can be self-sustaining

Knowledge check 59

What do you think are the most important influences on the positioning strategy adopted by a business such as Apple?

The difficulties of maintaining a competitive advantage

Sustaining competitive advantage can be difficult for business. This is due to:

- Maintaining product differentiation – competitors will attempt to copy successful business ideas and/or improve them. This means that the business may lose its USP.
- New entrants to the market – as well as existing competitors, new rivals may be attracted by the increased sales and profits generated by a successful business idea.
- Changes in fashion and consumer taste – in fast-changing markets such as music, fashion and mobile phones, product life cycles are short. Consequently, unless a business is consistently able to bring out innovative products, it may lose its competitive advantage over its rivals.

Knowledge check 60

Identify three ways a business can sustain its competitive advantage.

Exam tip

Remember to refer to the stimulus material when answering questions on the factors that could affect the competitive advantage of the business featured.

Summary

In this section you should be able to:
- Define competitive advantage.
- Understand the importance of strategic positioning.
- Explain Porter's low-cost, differentiation and focus strategies.
- Relate Porter's theory to real-life business examples.
- Explain Bowman's strategic clock.
- Appreciate the strengths and weaknesses of Porter's generic strategies theory.
- Consider the benefits and limitations of Bowman's strategic clock.
- Understand the influences that determine the strategic positioning of a business.
- Explain the benefits resulting from a business achieving a position of competitive advantage.
- Understand the difficulties for a business in sustaining its position of competitive advantage.

Questions & Answers

A-level Business will consist of three exam papers.

Paper 1 consists of three compulsory sections:
- Section A: 15 multiple-choice questions (15 marks in total)
- Section B: short-answer questions (35 marks in total)
- Sections C and D: two essay questions (choice of one from two and one from two), both worth 25 marks (50 marks in total).

Paper 2 consists of:
- three data-response compulsory questions worth approximately 33 marks each and made up of three- or four-part questions (100 marks in total).

Paper 3 consists of:
- an extended case study including appendices containing data. There are six questions of increasing levels of difficulty (100 marks in total).

This section of the guide contains the various types of exam questions that you are likely to be faced with. In the exam, the papers can contain questions from the entire specification. The questions in this guide are based upon only section 1.7: 'Analysing the strategic position of a business' and section 1.8: 'Choosing strategic direction'. The correct answers for the multiple-choice questions are supplied together with comments on why these answers are correct. For the short-answer, data-response, case study and essay questions you will find sample answers with comments. Student 'A' sample answer is a good response and Student 'B' is a weak response – the aim being to illustrate common errors made by students and examples of good practice in the hope that you will, with practice, be able to develop your own skills.

Questions

Since the multiple-choice and short-answer questions give a broad coverage of the content of this book it would make sense to use these towards the end of your revision period in order to check your knowledge. The data-response questions, however, could be used as you complete an area of content. The Paper 3 questions are based upon different content sections in this book, but would be best answered towards the end of your revision.

Sample answers

Resist the temptation to study the answers before you have attempted the questions. If you make a mistake here it is not the end of the world and practice at developing your own responses will help you hone your skills. Once you have written your answer you can then look at the sample responses and identify the strengths and weaknesses of your own work. Using the question and answer section in this way should result in the quality of your answers improving.

Assessment

A-level papers do not just test how well you know the content of the subject. There is a clear set of skills that will be tested and it is essential that you are aware of these skills and have some idea of how to satisfy them.

The following skills are tested:

- Knowledge and understanding: this relates to the content of the specification and how well you know and understand the various business concepts, theories and ideas.
- Application: this focuses on your ability to relate your knowledge and understanding of the subject content to a particular situation or scenario (such as that in a particular case study).
- Analysis: this is the ability to develop an extended line of argument related to a particular question.
- Evaluation: this is making a judgement by weighing up the evidence provided.

Not all questions will test all the skills set out above so it is important that you are able to recognise which skills are being tested. The basis of all questions will be some element of knowledge, but the clue to the other skills required is in the command words of a question. Some commonly used ones are listed below.

Application

The following command words require you to apply your answer to the context of the question or case.

- 'Explain'
- 'Calculate'

Analyse

The following command words require you to develop a relevant argument. Remember this has to be in context and will need application also.

- 'Analyse'
- 'Explain why'
- 'Examine'

Evaluate

The following command words require you to make a judgement. Remember again that in an answer that requires evaluation, arguments must be developed (analysis) and they must also be in context (application):

- 'Evaluate'
- 'Discuss'
- 'To what extent'
- 'Justify'

The majority of students who have studied hard and who underperform do not do so because of a lack of knowledge but because of a lack of good examination technique. If you understand the skills that are being tested, recognise how to develop them and are prepared to practise them, you should do well.

Paper 1-type questions

Section A Multiple-choice questions

Question 1

Which one of the following is not an external influence on a corporate objective?

A   Competitors

B   Shareholders

C   Employees

D   The economy

Question 2

Which one of the following is a financial efficiency ratio?

A   Gearing

B   Inventory turnover

C   Return on capital employed

D   Current ratio

Question 3

Which one of the following is not a non-current asset?

A   Inventories

B   Property

C   Vehicles

D   Machinery

Question 4

Elkington's triple bottom line consists of which of the three Ps?

A   Price, Promotion, Product

B   Place, Profit, Position

C   People, Power, Politics

D   Profit, People, Planet

Question 5

The chancellor of the exchequer announces a rise in income tax. This is an example of:

A   Monetary policy

B   Supply-side policy

C   Fiscal policy

D   Exchange rate policy

Question 6

A business invests in a new piece of machinery that costs £10 million and is expected to last 5 years. It is expected to bring in additional revenue of £3 million each year but incur annual costs of £0.75 million. The average rate of return for the machinery over 5 years would be:

A   12.5%

B   2.5%

C   112.5%

D   10%

Question 7

According to Ansoff, Jaguar Land Rover selling vehicles in India is an example of:

A   Market development

B   Diversification

C   Market penetration

D   New product development

Question 8

Which one of the following is not an example of demographic change?

A   Urbanisation

B   Consumer lifestyle

C   Migration

D   E-commerce

Question 9

Extracts from the financial accounts of a company show:

Share capital	£3,120m
Reserves	£692m
Non-current liabilities	£1,172m

The gearing ratio for the company is:

A   37.5%

B   46%

C   23.5%

D   69.5%

Question 10

Waitrose offers its customers high-quality products and service. According to Porter this is an example of a:

A   Focus strategy

B   Low-cost strategy

C   Differentiation strategy

D   Corporate responsibility strategy

Question 11

Which one of the following is a strategic decision?

A   To expand into the Chinese market

B   To launch a 3-week advertising campaign

C   To launch the product in Shanghai

D   To offer a 'buy one get one free' promotion

Question 12

Which one of the following is a profitability ratio?

A   Current ratio

B   Return on capital employed

C   Inventory turnover

D   Payables days

Question 13

Which one of the following is not one of Porter's five forces?

A   Buyer power

B   Supplier power

C   Threat of substitutes

D   Changes in the economy

Question 14

A business invests in a new piece of machinery that costs £10 million and is expected to last 5 years. It is expected to bring in additional revenue of £3 million each year but incur annual costs of £0.75 million. The payback period would be:

A   3 years and 5.3 months

B   3 years and 4 months

C   4 years and 5.3 months

D   4 years and 1 month

Question 15

The Living Wage is an example of which type of legislation?

A   Competition law

B   Employment law

C   Environmental law

D   Health and safety

Answers to multiple-choice questions

Question 1

Correct answer C.

ⓔ Employees are an internal influence.

Question 2

Correct answer B.

ⓔ Inventory turnover measures how efficiently a business converts its stock into sales.

Question 3

Correct answer A.

ⓔ Inventories is a current asset as it lasts less than 12 months.

Question 4

Correct answer D.

ⓔ This measures business performance in terms of profit, but also its effect on society and the environment.

Question 5

Correct answer C.

e Fiscal policy is concerned with taxation and government spending.

Question 6

Correct answer B.

e Total return: 5 × 2.25 = 11.25m – initial cost of 10m = 1.25m.
Annual return = 1.25/5 = 0.25m. ARR = 0.25/10 × 100 = 2.5%.

Question 7

Correct answer A.

e Market development is selling an existing product – Jaguar cars – in a new market, India.

Question 8

Correct answer D.

e E-commerce is the buying and selling of products using the internet – it is an example of technological change.

Question 9

Correct answer C.

e Gearing = non-current liabilities/capital employed × 100. Correct answer:

1172/4984 × 100 = 23.5%

Question 10

Correct answer C.

e Differentiation is a marketing strategy based upon a USP of superior products and service.

Question 11

Correct answer A.

e Expansion into China would be a medium- to long-term decision, the other options are short term and tactical.

Question 12

Correct answer B.

e ROCE measures operating profit as a percentage of capital employed.

Question 13

Correct answer D.

ℯ Changes in the economy could be considered either as a threat or an opportunity but is not part of Porter's five forces.

Question 14

Correct answer C.

ℯ Payback = 4 years plus 1/2.25 × 12 = 5.33 months.

Question 15

Correct answer B.

ℯ The Living Wage is legislation concerned with employees' entitlements related to their pay.

Section B Short-answer questions

Question 16

Year	Cash inflow	Cash outflow	Discount factor
0		200,000	1.00
1	100,000	50,000	0.91
2	150,000	50,000	0.83
3	175,000	50,000	0.75

Based on the data above, calculate the net present value. (4 marks)

ℯ 'Calculate' questions simply require you to perform a calculation. It is important to show all your workings as you may get marks for them even if your final answer is incorrect. There is no need to analyse your calculation.

Student A

Year	Net return	Present value
0	(200,000)	(200,000)
1	50,000	50,000 × 0.91 = 45,500
2	100,000	100,000 × 0.83 = 83,000
3	125,000	125,000 × 0.75 = 93,750

Net present value = 222,250 – 200,000 = 22,250.

ℯ **4/4 marks awarded.** Correct calculation of present values using the net return figures. Initial cost of 200,000 subtracted from total of present values to give the correct answer. All workings shown clearly.

Student B

Year 0	(200,000)
Year 1	100,000 × 0.91 = 91,000
Year 2	150,000 × 0.83 = 124,500
Year 3	175,000 × 0.75 = 131,250

Net present value = 346,750.

e **1/4 marks awarded.** Incorrect calculation of present values as cash inflow rather than net return figures have been used. Also net present value is incorrect as the initial cost of 200,000 has not been subtracted.

Question 17

Explain one possible benefit of a policy of corporate social responsibility for a food manufacturer.

(4 marks)

e 'Explain' questions require you to identify a point and then write a sentence that develops this point. Often it is a good idea to use an example to illustrate your explanation.

Student A

Corporate social responsibility (CSR) is when a business does more than what is required by the law in treating all of its stakeholders such as employees, customers and suppliers. For example, a food manufacturer may use Fairtrade suppliers who are paid a good price for their products. A benefit of this is that the manufacturer should get good-quality supplies, enabling it to produce consistently high-quality products and develop a good reputation.

e **4/4 marks awarded.** Correct definition of CSR. A relevant benefit is explained using the context of a food manufacturer.

Student B

Corporate social responsibility is 'doing the right thing'. It means a business makes decisions based on morals rather than profit. This is good because it gives the business more customers.

e **2/4 marks awarded.** The definition shows some understanding of CSR, but confuses it with the idea of ethics. A benefit is identified but not explained using the context of a food manufacturer.

Question 18

Explain one way in which an increase in interest rates could affect a building construction business.

(5 marks)

ⓔ This question asks you to explain one way a rise in interest rates could affect a building construction business. Do not waste time by explaining more than one point as you will not gain any extra marks.

Student A

Interest rates are the cost of borrowing. A rise in interest rates could have a negative effect on the sales of a building construction business. This is because buildings such as houses and factories are expensive and are usually paid for through borrowing loans or mortgages. If borrowing becomes too expensive, consumers will not be able to afford these loans and consequently the demand will fall.

ⓔ **5/5 marks awarded.** Correct definition of interest rates is provided. A relevant problem for a building construction business is identified and clearly explained.

Student B

Interest rates measure how much it costs to borrow. A rise in interest rates means that consumers may decide to save more. This means that they will spend less, resulting in less sales for the building business.

ⓔ 2/5 marks awarded. Correct understanding shown of interest rates and a relevant effect of rising interest rates identified. However, the explanation is limited and not related enough to the context of a building construction business.

Question 19

A supermarket is facing increased competition from online retailers. Analyse how it could use Porter's five forces to improve its competitiveness. (9 marks)

ⓔ 'Analyse' questions require you to develop a line of argument. You should aim to write at least two consecutive sentences that provide a well-developed chain of argument with no missing links. You should also aim to write in context by applying your argument to the type of business featured in the question.

Student A

Porter's five forces is used by a business to assess its external environment in terms of existing competitors, potential competitors, substitute products, suppliers and customers. It enables it to determine which of these pose the greatest opportunity or threat and then to devise a suitable strategy.

A supermarket facing increased competition from an online retailer could be considered a threat from a substitute product. Due to the low barriers of entry, the online retailer could be a major threat to the supermarket. In order to maintain its competitiveness, the supermarket would need to devise a strategy based upon the advantages it offers customers compared to the online retailer. For example, it could improve its customer service and improve the layout of its stores. This could develop a USP for the supermarket, ensuring that it attracts customers away from the online retailer.

ⓔ **9/9 marks awarded.** This is an excellent answer that reveals good understanding of Porter's five forces. It concludes a well-developed line of argument analysing how a supermarket could use this theory to develop a strategy to maintain its competitiveness with effective use of relevant examples.

Student B

Porter's five forces can be used by a business to analyse its external environment. If a supermarket is facing increased competition from online retailers, it needs to devise a strategy to defeat them. For example, it could lower its prices or spend more on advertising. This would result in it gaining more sales and profits.

ⓔ **3/9 marks awarded.** This answer shows some understanding of Porter's five forces. It identifies a relevant strategy that a business could adopt, but the analysis is limited and fails to effectively use the context of a supermarket.

Question 20

Analyse how a business operating in the social media market would benefit from the use of SWOT analysis in deciding upon a new strategy. (9 marks)

ⓔ Remember to read the question. This question asks you to analyse the benefits of SWOT analysis. Do not waste time considering the limitations of SWOT analysis.

Student A

SWOT analysis is a technique that a business can use to identify its internal strengths and weaknesses as well as external opportunities and threats.

One benefit of this technique is that it can identify potential threats and devise a strategy to counter them. A technological market such as social media is fast changing and relatively easy for new businesses to enter. As a result, new competitors could be a constant threat to the business. In order to counter the threat of new competition, the business could implement a strategy of product development, for example by adding new features to its website, in order to retain its market share.

Another benefit of SWOT analysis is that potential opportunities can be spotted and new services developed to exploit them. For example, the increased popularity of smartphones has led to more customers using them to buy products online. The business could exploit this by developing blogs and forums on its website to help its customers review products. This could enhance the reputation of the business and attract more users.

ⓔ **9/9 marks awarded.** This answer shows good understanding of SWOT analysis. It identifies two correct benefits, both of which are well explained. There is consistent reference to the context of the social media market, which would result in high marks for application.

Student B

SWOT analysis stands for strengths, weaknesses, opportunities and threats. It would benefit the business as it can enable the business to identify its strengths and use them to exploit any opportunities in the social media market. For example, if the business employs creative software designers, it could use them to design new apps.

Another benefit is that it can identify any weaknesses and then try to improve them. For example, if the company has an unfashionable image, it could complete some market research to find out why and then devise a new marketing campaign.

e **4/9 marks awarded.** This answer reveals correct understanding of SWOT analysis. It identifies two correct benefits and there is some explanation of each one. The first benefit makes some use of the context of the social media market, but the second benefit does not.

Section C Essay questions

You will have a choice of two questions in both sections C and D. You should write your answer in continuous prose and use examples to illustrate your answer.

Question 21

To what extent will changes in the political and legal environment provide an opportunity or a threat to a soft drinks manufacturer?   (25 marks)

e Essay questions require you to show all the skills of knowledge, application, analysis and evaluation. It is important that you spend time writing an essay plan before you start writing. A good essay structure is essential. Aim to write an introduction, two paragraphs that consider the opportunities, followed by two paragraphs considering the threats. Each paragraph should contain a separate argument that is well developed and uses the context of the business featured in the question. Complete your essay by writing a conclusion that directly answers the question and is supported by your previous arguments.

Student A

The political and legal environment includes areas such as consumer, employment and environmental legislation. Laws are made by politicians often in response to public pressure. It is important that business is aware of changes in the political and legal environment as these can present both opportunities and threats.

An example of a current issue facing soft drinks manufacturers is the bad publicity they are facing regarding the high levels of sugar in their products. Famous personalities like Jamie Oliver have started a campaign trying to persuade the government to put extra taxes on sugary drinks. This could be viewed as a potential threat to soft drinks manufacturers as extra taxes would

→

increase the price of their drinks. This could lead to a fall in sales and profits. Furthermore, the link of high sugar to obesity would create bad publicity and politicians may pass laws banning these drinks.

However, soft drinks manufacturers could view this as an opportunity. For example, they could develop low-sugar drinks such as Diet Coke or add healthier drinks to their product range such as bottled water. Coca-Cola anticipated this trend in recent years and exploited it by becoming a major shareholder of Innocent smoothies. This has improved its reputation and means that it is no longer dependent upon sugary drinks as its main source of sales.

Another change in the political and legal environment is the Living Wage. This means that employers must pay their workers at least £7.85 an hour. This is a threat to business as it will increase labour costs. If the business increases its prices to cover these increased costs it could lead to a fall in sales, particularly if the product has price-elastic demand. Also, if the business is competing against foreign competitors with lower labour costs, this could lead to a competitive disadvantage.

However, soft drinks manufacturers could respond by making their production more capital intensive. Investment in machinery could result in better quality, productivity and increased output. With fewer employees, a rise in wage costs would not have a significant effect. The majority of soft drinks manufacturers are capital intensive, so the Living Wage should not be a major issue for them. Also, if they employ skilled workers to maintain the machinery, manufacturers should offer good pay and conditions. The benefits from this could include lower labour turnover, less absenteeism and a reputation as a good employer.

In conclusion, many businesses view changes in the political and legal environment as a threat. This is due to the fact that they could lead to increased costs and restrictions on business activities. It is important that business is constantly aware of these changes and develops strategies that can counter these threats. Forward-thinking companies anticipate these changes and are able to use them to exploit opportunities that may result.

ⓔ **25/25 marks awarded.** This response reveals good understanding of the political and legal environment. It identifies two key issues that are relevant to the context of a soft drinks manufacturer. Each of these is well developed with effective lines of argument. The conclusion brings together the key issues and provides a judgement that directly answers the question.

Student B

The legal environment includes all the laws that businesses have to follow. These include health and safety and equal opportunities.

A threat to a soft drinks manufacturer could be a change in environmental laws. For example, there could be extra penalties for businesses that cause pollution. The manufacturer would have to spend money on waste treatment facilities which would increase its costs. Also the business may have to use less packaging or use materials that are recyclable.

Another threat could be an increase in health and safety. For a soft drinks manufacturer this means that it has to spend more money on training its workers, buying safety clothing and making sure that the machinery is not dangerous. This increase in costs will mean less profits.

An opportunity from changes in the legal environment could be from equal opportunities. If a business does not discriminate between different workers it could gain a good reputation. This means that there will be high levels of motivation, leading to better quality and productivity.

Another opportunity could be from changes in consumer law. If a business charges fair prices and gives its customers good guarantees for its products, it will get a good image. This will mean that the business will get more sales and profits.

In conclusion, changes in the legal environment can mean both threats and opportunities for a business. The threats could include having to spend more money reducing pollution and improving health and safety. The opportunities could be a better reputation for being a good employer and treating customers well.

📝 **12/25 marks awarded.** This answer shows understanding of the legal environment but not the political. It identifies relevant issues regarding legislation and there is an attempt at times to relate this to the context of a soft drinks manufacturer. There is an attempt to explain the effects of legislation in terms of opportunities or threats, but the analysis is simplistic with many assumptions. There is a lack of focus on 'changes' in the political and legal environment, resulting in this answer not directly answering the question. The conclusion simply summarises the previous points and so fails to answer the question.

Question 22

To what extent would a strategy of market development be the best way to increase business profits?

(25 marks)

📝 In this essay you should consider arguments that support the statement that market development is the best way to increase business profits, followed by counter arguments. These could be related to either the problems of a market development strategy and/or an alternative strategy. Each argument needs to be well developed and illustrated with business examples. Your essay should finish with a conclusion that directly answers the question and is supported by your previous arguments.

Market development is a strategy of launching an existing product into a new market. This could be a new country or a different market segment. Market development is part of Ansoff's matrix, which is used to assess the degree of risk and reward associated with a particular strategy.

The reward from market development is the opportunity to target a new market which could be more profitable than an existing one. The German supermarket Aldi is a good example of a business that has successfully used market development to increase its profits. Aldi has rapidly increased its sales and market share of the UK supermarket sector. Due to its ability to minimise costs, Aldi was able to charge much lower prices than rivals such as Tesco and Asda. Aldi's stores are much smaller and have cheaper locations. They also offer a more limited product range. This means that its costs are lower, enabling Aldi to charge lower prices. The UK economy is only slowly coming out of recession and consumers are still very conscious of how much they can afford to spend. Aldi exploited this by quickly recognising the importance of low prices to UK customers. This illustrates how market development can lead to increased profits.

However, there is also greater risk with market development because the business is selling its products to an unknown market. As a result, it is important that a business conducts extensive market research before it enters a new market. For example, Tesco failed in the USA with its 'Fresh 'n' Easy' stores because it failed to recognise that US customers had different tastes. For example, US customers expect high levels of customer service, such as employees helping them with their packing at the checkouts. Tesco failed to provide this, resulting in customer complaints and a poor reputation. As a result, its US stores failed, costing Tesco millions of pounds. This example illustrates that market development is not always the best way to increase profits.

An alternative strategy to increase profits is market penetration, by selling existing products to an existing market. A business that has increased its profits with this strategy is John Lewis. Its stores are popular because of the excellent customer service and good-quality products. John Lewis has been successful and increased its profits through opening more stores in the UK. It understands what its customers want and consistently provides high quality. As a result, it has developed a good reputation, high levels of brand loyalty and can charge high prices. This shows that market development is not the only way to increase profits.

In conclusion, it is not true that market development is the best way to increase profits. For a company like Aldi, it has proved to be successful, but this was due to the fact that Aldi understood its new market and provided a product that was superior to the existing competition. Tesco failed to do this and as a consequence suffered heavy losses. For some businesses, such as John Lewis, a better way to increase profits is simply to focus on increasing market share in an existing market.

ⓔ **25/25 marks awarded.** This is an excellent answer. It reveals good understanding of market development. Relevant arguments for and against this strategy are well developed, with detailed use of business examples for illustration. An alternative strategy for increasing profits is also identified and fully analysed with the use of a detailed example.

Student B

Market development is when a business sells an existing product to a new market. It is part of Ansoff's matrix which considers how much risk there is with a business strategy.

A business that has used market development to increase its profits is Aldi. This is a German supermarket that is very popular in England. Aldi has gained high sales because it is much cheaper than rivals such as Tesco and Sainsbury's. Because of the recession, consumers had less money to spend so were attracted by Aldi's low prices.

Another business that has used market development to increase its profits is Jaguar Land Rover (JLR). It has been very successful in countries like China and India. The economy in these countries is growing and means that there are now more customers who can afford to buy expensive cars. Most of JLR's sales are now in India and China.

A business that failed when using market development was Tesco. It entered the US market by buying the 'Fresh 'n' Easy' supermarket chain. However, Tesco failed because it did not do enough market research to find out what US customers wanted. The stores in the USA only made poor sales and Tesco sold them off, which cost it millions of pounds.

In conclusion, market development can increase profits as long as you have a product that consumers like and you have done enough research. Entering a new market is risky and there is a greater chance of failure, as shown by Tesco.

ⓔ **13/25 marks awarded.** This answer shows good understanding of market development. It contains relevant arguments of both the advantages and disadvantages of market development and illustrates these with useful business examples. However, both the analysis and the amount of detail regarding each example are only reasonable. Furthermore, alternative strategies to increase profits are not considered.

The conclusion simply summarises the previous arguments and fails to directly answer the question as to whether market development is the 'best' way to increase profits.

Section D Essay questions

Question 23

To what extent do you think a business should focus on the needs of its shareholders rather than its other stakeholders?

(25 marks)

ℯ In this essay you need to show good understanding of the different stakeholders that a business has to consider. You should aim to write two paragraphs that identify and explain separate arguments why a business should consider shareholders' needs first. A business example should be used to illustrate at least one of your arguments. You should then aim to write two further paragraphs, each of which identifies and explains arguments why other stakeholders' needs should be considered. Use a business example to illustrate your argument. Finally, you should write a conclusion that directly answers the question and is supported by your previous arguments.

Student A

A stakeholder is an individual or group that has an effect on or is affected by the activities of an organisation. Stakeholders include shareholders, employees, customers and suppliers.

One argument why a business should consider shareholders' needs first is that they are the owners of the business. Without the finance provided by shareholders, the business may not exist. In return for their investment, shareholders expect good returns, specifically high dividends and a rising share price. Consequently, the business should concentrate on maximising profits in order to provide good shareholder returns. The shareholder concept argues that by focusing solely on generating good profits, the business can concentrate on improving efficiency and achieving high sales. It considers that having to consider other stakeholders' interests will distract the business from achieving high profitability and could lead to increased costs and slower decision making. For example, Primark generates good profits because its focus on efficiency enables it to charge competitive prices. If it provided its employees with better pay and conditions, this could lead to higher costs, forcing Primark to charge higher prices. Consequently, it could lose its competitive advantage, resulting in lower profits and returns for shareholders.

Another argument why shareholders' needs should be put first is that the business may gain a good reputation with existing and potential investors. A business that consistently provides impressive shareholder returns will benefit if it wishes to raise additional finance through selling shares, as there will be plenty of investors keen to buy them. Share capital has the advantage compared to borrowing of avoiding the cost of interest payments as well as higher gearing levels.

However, the stakeholder concept argues that business success is dependent upon meeting the needs of all stakeholders. For example, a business that provides its employees with good pay and conditions could gain a number of benefits. These include higher productivity, better quality and customer service, all of which contribute to improved profitability. John Lewis is a good example of a business that places high priority on its employees' needs. It provides good pay and conditions, as well as a generous profit share scheme. As a result, its motivated employees provide high levels of customer service, enabling John Lewis to benefit from a good reputation. Consequently, the business attracts many customers who are happy to pay high prices, enabling John Lewis to generate good profits.

→

Another stakeholder that contributes to business success is suppliers. Manufacturing businesses that employ just in time (JIT) are heavily dependent upon reliable suppliers. If suppliers are given long-term contracts, fair prices and are paid promptly, they should in return provide reliable delivery of good-quality components. As a result, the business will benefit from the operational efficiencies that result from JIT.

In conclusion, ultimately the business should consider the needs of shareholders first because they are the owners. However, the profits required to provide shareholder returns are dependent upon the effective contribution of other stakeholders. Consequently, a successful business will recognise the importance of meeting the interests of key stakeholders such as employees and suppliers as well as those of the shareholders.

ⓔ **25/25 marks awarded.** This is an excellent response. It shows good understanding of stakeholders. Two relevant arguments for meeting shareholders' needs are well explained and illustrated with a relevant business example. This is followed by two valid counter arguments, each of which is well explained and illustrated with relevant business examples.

The conclusion answers the question and is supported by the previous arguments.

Student B

Stakeholders are the different groups of people who are interested in the activities of a business. They include shareholders, customers, employees and the local community.

Shareholders want the business to make good profits. This means that the business can then afford to give them good dividends. Also, if the share price goes up, they can sell their shares for a profit. If the shareholders are unhappy with the amount of profits made by the business they can sack the directors. This happened last year when Tesco made poor profits and the chief executive was forced to resign. This shows that it is important to keep shareholders happy.

Another reason is that if you think about other stakeholders' needs it could increase your costs and reduce profits. If a business spent more money on reducing pollution, it would please the local community but costs would rise and there would be no increase in sales. This means the business would make less profit.

One reason why you should not meet shareholders' needs is that other stakeholders are also important. If a business does not keep its customers happy by charging fair prices, it could get a bad reputation and lose sales. Some football clubs have been accused of charging too much for season tickets and as a result have lost supporters who refuse to pay the high prices.

In conclusion, a business should consider its shareholders first because they own the business and can sack the directors if they do not get good returns. However, it is important to consider other stakeholders as well.

ⓔ 12/25 marks awarded. This answer shows good understanding of stakeholders. It provides two valid arguments why a business should consider its shareholders and there is a reasonable explanation of each. The use of Tesco is also a relevant example, but more detail is needed.

The answer includes a counter argument which is reasonably explained using a relevant example. However, another counter argument would have given the answer more breadth.

The conclusion is too brief and simply summarises the previous arguments.

Question 24

To what extent are mission statements crucial for effective business strategic decision making?

(25 marks)

ⓔ This essay requires you to show an understanding of mission statements and you should write two well-developed reasons why mission statements are crucial for strategic decision making. Aim to illustrate at least one of your arguments with a relevant business example.

You should then aim to write two separate paragraphs, each of which contains well-developed counter arguments regarding how crucial mission statements are for strategic decision making. Try to illustrate these arguments with business examples.

Your conclusion must directly answer the question and focus upon the extent to which mission statements are crucial, based upon your previous analysis.

Student A

A mission statement is an attempt by a business to put its aims into words that will motivate its employees to work towards achieving these aims. It should give employees a sense of direction and ensure that all functional areas of the business are working together in order to achieve the same goal.

One reason why mission statements are crucial for strategic business decision making is that the mission statement is the foundation upon which strategic decisions are made. The mission statement will often state what the business ultimately wants to achieve. For example, if a business aims to be 'the market leader for confectionery', it can then set specific objectives that need to be achieved, e.g. increase market share to 20% by 2020. This then enables objectives to be set for each functional area, which each contribute to the corporate objective. Once objectives have been set, the business can then decide upon the required strategy to achieve them. Without the mission statement, the business would lack focus and a sense of direction.

For example, Facebook's mission is to 'give people the power to share and make the world more open and connected'. Facebook can then set specific objectives such as increasing the number of its subscribers in emerging economies by a certain percentage. →

Another reason why mission statements are crucial for decision making is that they give employees a sense of direction. This is particularly true in multinational corporations employing thousands of people all over the world. A clear mission statement that expresses what the business stands for and what it aims to achieve enables all employees to understand what they are all working towards. This should result in better communication and coordination between all the multinational's regional operations across the world. Ultimately the success of any business strategy in achieving its objectives is dependent upon the employees carrying it out effectively. Without a mission statement, employees will be confused regarding what the business is trying to achieve and consequently may lack commitment.

However, in many cases, mission statements are badly written and hard to understand. As a result, the various business stakeholders may be confused regarding what the business is aiming to achieve. This could lead to unrealistic objectives being set and inappropriate strategies. Often mission statements are just viewed as a public relations exercise and not taken seriously by employees. The opportunity cost spent on writing meaningless mission statements can be considerable, especially as they are often composed by senior managers, whose time could be better spent on strategic decision making.

Another problem is that a business can gain a bad reputation if its actions do not correspond with the values stated in its mission statement. A famous example is Google, whose mission statement is to 'organise the world's information and make it universally accessible and useful'. When Google entered China it had to agree to censorship by the Chinese government, resulting in information being restricted to Chinese people. This contradicted its mission statement and as a result Google suffered from a bad reputation as well as many of its employees feeling let down by the business. In this case the value of the mission statement in strategic decision making was diminished because Google had undermined its values through its actions in China.

Overall, the extent to which a mission statement is crucial to strategic decision making is dependent upon how well it states the aims of the business and how effectively it acts as a foundation for setting objectives and strategy. A well-written mission statement that is clearly understood, provides a sense of direction to employees and is backed up by actions from senior management is a powerful way to ensure a business can achieve its aims. However, without these elements, mission statements can be meaningless and could actually contribute to business failure.

e **20/25 marks awarded.** This answer provides a correct definition of mission statements. It identifies two relevant arguments that clearly explain the value of mission statements in strategic decision making. Each of these is well developed. A relevant business example is used, but another example would have added more depth.

Two counter arguments are also identified and well explained. A relevant business example is used to illustrate one of the arguments.

The conclusion directly answers the question and is supported by the previous arguments.

Student B

A mission statement states what the business hopes to achieve in the long run. It includes things like its aims and what it stands for.

An advantage of a mission statement is that it gives the business a sense of direction. This means that all the employees understand what the business is hoping to achieve. As a result, employees will be more motivated and will work harder to achieve objectives. A good example of a mission statement is Virgin: 'Our vision is to contribute to creating happy and fulfilling lives which are also sustainable – surely a vision worth aspiring to? With businesses spanning many sectors and touching many aspects of our customers' lifestyles we feel that Virgin is in a perfect position to contribute to this vision. After all, the Virgin brand has always been about having fun in a unique Virgin way.' Employees who work for Virgin will understand what the business is about and will be motivated to work for it.

Another advantage of a mission statement is that it informs customers about what its values are. This could be a good way to promote the business and attract consumers. For example, if a business says that it aims to be more ethical and good for the environment, consumers may agree with this and deliberately buy its products. Companies like Innocent Drinks and Ben & Jerry's have benefited from having mission statements which are to do with being socially responsible.

A disadvantage of a mission statement is that they are confusing and hard to understand. Because of this they are not taken seriously. Often a mission statement is too long and does not mean anything. Employees will then be demotivated because they do not understand what the business stands for and what they are working to achieve. As a result, labour turnover and absenteeism will rise.

Also many mission statements are just seen as a public relations exercise and are not taken seriously by the senior managers. This can often then result in the business gaining bad publicity. A good example of this happened to the Co-op, whose mission statement is concerned with being socially responsible and having good ethics. However, one of its senior managers was uncovered by the media to be taking illegal drugs and other corrupt behaviour. As a result, the Co-op gained a bad reputation and many customers stopped shopping there because they felt let down.

To conclude, mission statements have both advantages and disadvantages. The advantages are that they can motivate employees because it gives them a sense of direction and also attract customers who agree with their values. The disadvantages are that they are often too long and confusing. Also, if senior managers do not behave in the same way as the values in the mission statement, the business will gain bad publicity.

ⓔ **12/25 marks awarded.** This response shows some understanding of mission statements. It contains relevant arguments regarding both the benefits and limitations of mission statements, which are reasonably well explained and illustrated with valid business examples. However, the weakness of this response is that it fails to directly answer the question. Instead of discussing how crucial mission statements are to business decision making, this response simply describes the advantages and disadvantages of mission statements. As a result, the conclusion fails to address the question and simply summarises the previous arguments. Remember, in the exam it is important to ensure that you fully understand what the question is asking you to do. Make sure that you spend time thinking about the question and planning your answer before you start writing.

Paper 2-type data-response questions

Question 1

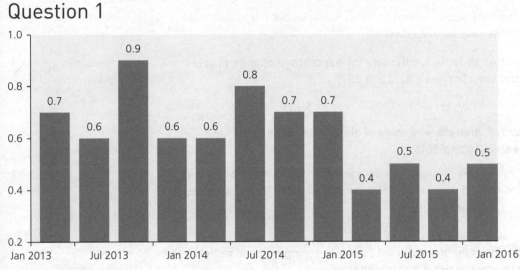

Figure 1 UK GDP growth rate

Source: www.tradingeconomics.com, Office for National Statistics

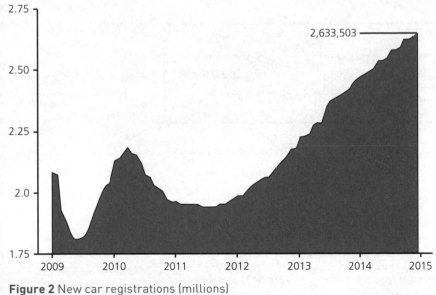

Figure 2 New car registrations (millions)

Source: SMMT (www.tinyurl.com/jogy66b)

Questions & Answers

Table 1 Electric cars in the UK, 2013–15

	2013	2014	2015
UK sales of electric cars	3,500	12,000	48,000
Average UK fuel price/litre	£1.35	£1.28	£1.10
Average price of an electric car	£25,000	£23,000	£20,000

(a) Describe one key feature of the data shown in Figure 1. (3 marks)

 'Describe' questions ask you to identify a trend from the data. It is also useful to carry out any calculations that are relevant.

(b) Using the information in Table 1, calculate the percentage change in sales revenue of electric cars between 2013 and 2015. (3 marks)

 Remember to show all your workings for calculation questions.

(c) Using the data above, analyse why sales of electric vehicles in the UK increased between 2013 and 2015. (9 marks)

 Remember to always refer to the actual data when answering the question. Also try to identify any links between the different sets of data. This will enable you to score highly for 'application' as well as provide evidence upon which to base your analysis.

(d) To what extent do you think a greater focus on producing electric vehicles should be the strategy for all UK car manufacturers? (20 marks)

 For 20-mark questions, you need to provide an argument both for and against the proposed strategy followed by a supported conclusion that directly answers the question.

Student A

(a) The data show that GDP has grown during the period 2013–15, indicating that the economy is in the recovery stage of the business cycle. The trend indicates that the rate of growth has declined between 2013 and 2015, falling from an average of 0.7% in 2013 to 0.5% in 2015.

 **3/3 marks awarded.** This response provides more detail by making actual use of the data and draws a conclusion from it.

Student B

(a) It shows that GDP growth was higher in 2013 and then fell in both 2014 and 2015.

 **1/3 marks awarded.** This is a correct identification of a feature of the data, but no attempt is made to describe this effectively.

Student A

(b) Sales revenue 2013: 3,500 × 25,000 = 87.5 million

Sales revenue 2015: 48,000 × 20,000 = 960 million

% change = $\dfrac{960 - 87.5}{87.5}$ × 100 = 997%

ⓔ **3/3 marks awarded.** Correct answer with all calculations shown.

Student B

(b) Sales revenue 2013: 3,500 × 25,000 = 87.5 million

Sales revenue 2015: 48,000 × 20,000 = 960 million

% change = $\dfrac{960}{87.5}$ = 10.97

ⓔ **1/3 marks awarded.** Correct calculation of sales for each year but no attempt to calculate the amount sales have risen and express this figure as a percentage.

Student A

(c) The data in Figure 1 indicate that the economy is now in the recovery stage of the business cycle as GDP is growing, although only slowly. During the recovery stage, consumers begin to feel more confident and are prepared to spend more on positive income elastic products such as cars.

The data in Figure 2 confirm this as sales of new cars have risen from roughly 2.1 million in 2013 to 2.6 million in 2015. This figure is for all cars, but sales of electric cars have risen from 3,500 to 48,000 during this period. Although this represents only 1.8% of all car sales in 2015 (48,000/2.6 million × 100), the figures indicate that consumers are now more interested in buying electric cars. As well as the environmental benefits from owning an electric car, the fall in price from £25,000 to £20,000 could be a reason for their increased popularity. This indicates that demand for electric cars is also price elastic.

ⓔ **9/9 marks awarded.** This answer effectively links all the data to provide reasons for the increased sales of electric cars. It makes good use of theory to develop arguments through the use of concepts such as the business cycle, income and price elasticity. It also uses relevant calculations to support the arguments.

Student B

(c) Because GDP is growing, as shown in Figure 1, this means that people have more money to spend on luxuries such as cars. Figure 2 shows that sales of cars have risen to 2.6 million, meaning that more people can afford new cars. Table 1 shows that electric cars are also more popular, with sales rising from 3,500 in 2013 to 48,000 in 2015. This could be because the price has dropped from £25,000 to £20,000.

ⓔ 3/9 marks awarded. This answer identifies relevant points from the data, but simply describes them with limited explanation and no use of relevant theory.

Student A

(d) There are arguments both for and against whether a greater focus on producing electric vehicles should be the strategy for all UK car manufacturers.

An argument for electric vehicles is that they are becoming more popular, as shown by sales growing by 997% between 2013 and 2015. This is an impressive rate of growth and indicates that this market has great potential. As the economy slowly begins to recover, consumer confidence rises and spending on luxuries such as cars should rise. The data in Figure 2 showing the rising trend in new car sales prove this. More consumers are now interested in purchasing electric cars because of their environmental benefits and lower running costs. Car manufacturers can exploit this by producing vehicles that emphasise these benefits and use them as a USP. Porter would argue that this could be considered a differentiation strategy and attract consumers.

However, an argument against electric vehicles is that it is still a niche market. Only 48,000 out of 2.6 million new cars in 2015 were electric. This represents just 1.8% of the market. Car manufacturers may have to spend significant amounts of money developing electric cars, which may generate only small returns. This could mean longer payback and low average rate of return. Also, the fall in petrol prices indicates that the economic benefits of owning an electric car are not so attractive for consumers. Consequently, in the short term, a strategy to make more electric vehicles may not be the best one for all UK car manufacturers.

In conclusion, I would consider that in the short term a greater focus on electric vehicles is not the best strategy for all UK car manufacturers. This is because the market is currently not big enough and greater profits can be made from petrol vehicles. However, in the long term, if electric vehicles become more popular, car manufacturers should seriously consider increasing their production.

ⓔ 20/20 marks awarded. This answer includes valid arguments both for and against the increased production of electric vehicles. Each of these is well developed and makes effective use of the data. Effective use of theory such as Porter and investment appraisal is made to support the arguments.

The conclusion directly answers the question by making a judgement based upon the previous arguments.

Student B

(d) An argument for car manufacturers to make more electric vehicles is that they are becoming more popular. Sales have risen from 3,500 to 48,000. This shows that there is an opportunity to increase sales and profit. Also, as the economy recovers, more people can afford to buy electric cars, especially as they now cost only £20,000 compared with £25,000.

An argument against electric vehicles is that only a small number of consumers are interested in buying them. In 2015, 2.6 million cars were sold, of which only 48,000 were electric. This shows that car manufacturers can make more profits from selling petrol cars.

In conclusion, I think that car manufacturers should concentrate more on ordinary cars until electric ones become more popular.

ⓔ 7/20 marks awarded. This answer identifies relevant points both for and against producing electric vehicles. These points are illustrated with relevant data. However, the arguments are not well explained and the conclusion is not supported effectively by the previous arguments.

Question 2

Read the information below and then answer the questions that follow.

IKEA: the world's largest furniture retailer

IKEA achieved worldwide sales of £23 billion in 2015, a 5% increase from 2014. There were 771 million customer visits to its 328 stores across 28 countries. At this rate of progress, the company is well on track to achieve its objective of £36 billion sales by 2020.

China, which is home to eight of IKEA's ten largest stores, continues to be the biggest source of growth due to the mass movement of people to the cities and a fast-growing middle class who can afford to buy the company's products. Sales also continue to rise in Russia, North America and Europe. When a new store opened in Valencia, there were 250 applicants for each of the 400 available jobs.

IKEA's success is based upon the values of its founder, Ingvar Kamprad. He stressed the importance of a cost-conscious approach for improving the business, by encouraging practical ways to make the best use of the company's resources. Each employee is valued by the business and they are encouraged to work together to come up with new ideas. Recently the company announced that it would pay all its UK workers the 'Living Wage' of at least £7.85 per hour.

Furthermore, IKEA believes that its long-term profitability is based upon a strategy of corporate social responsibility. To quote: 'We strive to create shared value in relation to our primary stakeholders – franchisees, employees, customers and suppliers – and in relation to society.' It also has established the Kamprad Family Foundation, which each year aims to donate £20 million to 'support, stimulate and reward education and scientific research in a way promoting entrepreneurship, environment, competence, health and social progress'.

Questions & Answers

(a) Explain how Carroll's corporate social responsibility pyramid can be applied to IKEA. (6 marks)

ⓔ When a question asks you about a particular theory or concept, it is a good idea to start your answer with a definition of the theory/concept. A maximum of two arguments is sufficient for 6-mark questions.

(b) Analyse the importance of globalisation for a business such as IKEA. (9 marks)

ⓔ Remember that 'analysis' questions require you to make a well-developed line of argument for each point made. To gain 'application' marks you must support your argument with relevant data and/or data from the case study. There is no need to consider both sides of the argument and/or write a conclusion as this question would not have any marks for evaluation.

(c) To what extent do you think corporate social responsibility has been the main reason for IKEA's sales growth? (16 marks)

ⓔ The phrase 'To what extent' is commonly used for evaluation questions. Remember that these questions will require you to make arguments for and against followed by a supported judgement.

Student A

(a) Carroll's social responsibility pyramid shows the different stages that a business has to achieve in order to be considered a socially responsible business. IKEA has achieved all of these stages as firstly it has achieved its economic responsibilities by operating as a profitable business. This can be shown by achieving sales of £23 billion in 2015.

Secondly, it has achieved its legal responsibilities by meeting the legal requirements of each country that it operates in. For example, it has recently announced that all its UK workers will be paid the 'living wage' of at least £7.85 per hour. Thirdly, IKEA has met its ethical responsibilities through its policy of social responsibility, which means it treats all of its stakeholders well.

Finally, IKEA has achieved its philanthropic responsibilities through the Kamprad Family Foundation, which aims to donate £20 million each year to 'support, stimulate and reward education and scientific research in a way promoting entrepreneurship, environment, competence, health and social progress'.

ⓔ **6/6 marks awarded.** This answer reveals good understanding of Carroll's social responsibility model and provides relevant illustrations of how IKEA achieves it.

Student B

(a) This is a pyramid that shows what a business needs to do if it is to be socially responsible. It includes economic, legal and ethical.

IKEA is socially responsible because it makes good sales and profits. It also treats its employees well by paying them the 'living wage'.

---

e **3/6 marks awarded.** This answer shows some understanding of Carroll's social responsibility model. It makes a limited explanation of how IKEA achieves some of its elements, but this is incomplete.

Student A

(b) Globalisation means that business now operates in markets all over the world.

For IKEA this means that it has 328 stores in 28 countries, resulting in it achieving sales of £23 billion in 2015. The importance of globalisation means that it can sell its products all over the world, enabling it to increase its sales and profits. For example, IKEA has been particularly successful in China, with eight of its largest ten stores located there. China has a huge population and a growing middle class which IKEA has targeted. As a result, China has been responsible for most of IKEA's sales growth. This is important because IKEA is not dependent on one market – when sales fell in Europe and the USA, the increased revenue from China made up the difference.

Globalisation is also important for IKEA because it can employ workers from different cultural backgrounds. IKEA encourages its employees to come up with new ideas to improve the business. Employing workers from different cultural backgrounds could mean that IKEA benefits from a wider range of new ideas. Furthermore, the employees will have knowledge of the tastes and preferences of the customers from their country. This means that IKEA can adapt its products to these tastes, increasing the chances of it becoming more popular and increasing sales.

e **9/9 marks awarded.** This answer shows good understanding of globalisation. It provides two reasons why globalisation is important for IKEA, both of which are well analysed and illustrated with relevant examples from the case study.

Student B

(b) Globalisation is when products are sold all over the world.

It is important for IKEA because it means that it can now sell to a bigger market, meaning that it can increase sales and profits. Also selling in more markets means that IKEA's brand becomes more well known and it will not need to spend so much money on advertising.

Another reason is that IKEA can sell its markets in China, which has a large population, leading to increased sales and profits.

Finally, IKEA can employ people from different countries, meaning that it can gain lots of new ideas.

e **5/9 marks awarded.** This answer shows a reasonable understanding of globalisation. It identifies a number of reasons why globalisation is important for IKEA, but does not explain them or use examples from the case study.

Student A

(c) Corporate social responsibility (CSR) is when a business considers all of its stakeholders when making decisions. Stakeholders can include employees, shareholders and customers.

One argument for IKEA's policy of CSR being the main reason for its sales growth is the benefits resulting from a good reputation. For example, many consumers will approve of IKEA's intention to pay at least the 'Living Wage' to its UK workers. As a result, they may choose to go to IKEA rather than its rivals. This means that IKEA will benefit from this USP and as a result gain more sales and increase its market share. Furthermore, paying its employees well and encouraging them to come up with new ideas should lead to improved morale. This results in less absenteeism and lower labour turnover, meaning reduced recruitment and training costs. Also, happier employees in the IKEA stores may result in better customer service, which should enhance the reputation of the business.

An argument against CSR being the main reason for IKEA's sales growth is that consumers could be attracted to IKEA for other reasons. The case study states that the main source of growth has come from China. The huge population and growing numbers of middle-class customers who can afford to buy Western products are the reasons why sales have risen. There is no evidence that Chinese customers are interested in IKEA's CSR policy.

Overall I think that the sales growth is mainly due to the increased popularity of IKEA in China. In markets such as Europe and the USA, a policy of CSR may improve IKEA's reputation and attract customers, but these markets have not grown as fast as in China.

@ **16/16 marks awarded.** This answer shows good understanding of CSR. It identifies two relevant arguments, both well analysed. There is effective use of the case study to support and illustrate the arguments. The conclusion directly answers the question and is supported by the previous arguments.

Student B

(c) Corporate social responsibility is when a business acts ethically. This includes such things as treating employees well and not damaging the environment.

I think that being socially responsible has contributed to IKEA's sales growth because it will improve its reputation. Many consumers will choose to go to IKEA because of this rather than its competitors. This should lead to increased sales and market share.

However, it says in the case study that China has been the main source of its growth. This is because of its huge population and growing middle class who can afford IKEA's products.

In conclusion, I think that corporate social responsibility has not been the main reason for IKEA's sales growth because consumers are more interested in low prices than the environment.

e **7/16 marks awarded.** This answer shows some understanding of corporate social responsibility and identifies relevant arguments. There is some development of the arguments but only limited use of the case study.

The conclusion provides a judgement but this is not supported by the previous arguments. It is based upon opinion rather than evidence from the case study.

Paper 3-type compulsory case study question

Superdry

Superdry was formed in 2003. It is a clothing retailer that aims to sell affordable, premium-quality clothing. The business grew rapidly and was particularly popular with 20 to 24-year-old men. It became a public limited company in 2010 and used the funds raised from selling shares to finance its expansion plans. Currently Superdry has 573 stores or franchises spread over 69 countries and directly employs more than 3,900 employees.

Superdry's mission statement is: 'To offer our customers innovative, premium and affordable quality clothing and accessories.' Its overall aim is: 'To become a global lifestyle brand.'

Since becoming a plc, Superdry has encountered a number of problems. The business struggled to cope with its rapid expansion, resulting in stock control and distribution difficulties. During the economic recession, profits fell as consumers were unable to afford Superdry's higher prices and switched to cheaper rivals such as Primark and H&M. Furthermore, there were quality issues with some suppliers and the brand became less popular with its 20–24-year-old market. As a result, profits fell, disappointing shareholders, and two directors resigned.

Eaun Sutherland was appointed in 2014 as Superdry's new chief executive. He is responsible for devising a strategy to achieve the aim of making Superdry a global lifestyle brand and to provide long-term sustainable growth for the business. The strategy consists of the following elements:

- Embed – by developing a brand that remains popular for a long time. Superdry recently launched an 'Idris Elba' collection that is aimed at older male customers than its current 20–24 year olds.
- Enable – by investing in training employees, improving its IT systems and warehouse/distribution facilities.
- Extend – by developing its womenswear clothing as well as a new sportswear range. It also sells its products using a multi-channel approach, enabling customers to buy Superdry products from its stores or through its website.
- Execute – by opening more stores in Europe, the USA and China. Superdry has established a joint venture with a Chinese clothing company that owns 3,000 stores in China. 55% of Superdry's sales revenue comes from its overseas stores.

So far, the strategy has proved successful, with a rise in sales and profits in 2015 compared with the previous year. Superdry has adopted a strategic position in its market by offering products that appeal to customers who are interested in stylish clothes of good quality, priced higher than the average. To quote from Superdry's annual report: 'Our customers come from a broad background, are aspirational and interested in both style and quality.'

Appendix 1 Extracts from Superdry's 2015 accounts

Income statement:	£m
Revenue	486.6
Cost of sales	(190.4)
Operating profit	60.2

Balance sheet:	£m
Receivables	70.3
Payables	79.8
Capital employed	327

Appendix 3 UK customer profile

Age	%
Over 35	25
25–34	35
20–24	40

Income group	%
High	35
Middle	55
Low	10

Appendix 2 Selected ratios 2014

Return on capital employed	15.3%
Payables days	124 days
Receivables days	46 days

Question 1

Analyse the importance of Superdry's mission statement for its strategic decision making. (12 marks)

ⓔ Always remember to define the concept being examined in the question. Also keep focused on the question. In this case you need to focus on the importance of the mission statement for strategic decision making, rather than the general benefits of a mission statement.

Student A

A mission statement is used to state the aims of a business as well as its values. Superdry's aim is to 'become a global lifestyle brand'.

The mission statement is used as the starting point for deciding the objectives of the business and the strategy to achieve it. It gives the employees a sense of direction. This is particularly useful for a large organisation like Superdry that has 3,900 employees spread over 69 countries.

To achieve the aim of becoming a global lifestyle brand, Superdry can set specific objectives such as launching new products successfully and gaining market share in new markets. Euan Sutherland, the chief executive, can then decide upon the strategy to achieve this. For example, Superdry has entered a joint venture with a Chinese company in order to become popular in the Chinese market. Without a mission statement, Superdry would be unsure what it wanted to achieve and as a result set unrealistic objectives and the wrong strategy. Consequently, a mission statement is of great importance as it is the foundation upon which strategic decisions are made.

ⓔ **12/12 marks awarded.** This answer shows good understanding of a mission statement by starting with a correct definition. It then develops a strong chain of argument that analyses how the mission statement is the starting point for setting objectives and strategy. This argument is illustrated with relevant examples from the case study.

Student B

A mission statement is useful because it says what the business stands for and what it hopes to achieve. This is a good motivator for employees as they know what the business is doing. Superdry wants to 'offer our customers innovative, premium and affordable quality clothing and accessories'.

A mission statement is good because aims and objectives can then be set. Superdry wants to extend its womenswear clothing and also launch an Idris Elba collection. This should attract new customers and increase sales and profits, which will please the shareholders.

ⓔ **5/12 marks awarded.** This answer reveals some understanding of the purpose of a mission statement and identifies two relevant benefits. However, it fails to answer the question because it does not explain why it is important for strategic decision making. There is an attempt to use examples from the case study, but they are not used to support any relevant argument.

Question 2

Using the data in Appendices 1 and 2, do you think Superdry's shareholders will be pleased with its profitability and financial efficiency in 2015?   (16 marks)

ⓔ It is important that you use the data to make relevant calculations in order to gain good marks for application. The calculations will also enable you to make stronger analytical arguments. Remember that this question also requires you to show the skill of evaluation, as you have to directly answer whether or not specifically the shareholders will be pleased.

Student A

Profitability measures how well the business is generating profits from its assets. The best measure of profitability is the return on capital employed (ROCE). In 2015 the ROCE achieved by Superdry was:

$$60.2/327 \times 100 = 18.4\%$$

This compares to 15.3% achieved in 2014, an improvement of 3.1%. Shareholders will be pleased by this improved performance as the business is generating more profit from its assets. As a result, shareholders should benefit from an increased share price and increased dividends.

Financial efficiency can be measured by comparing receivables days with payables days. These ratios measure how well a business controls its cash flow by measuring how quickly it receives income from its customers in comparison with how long it takes to pay its creditors. ➡

For Superdry in 2015:

Receivables days = 70.3/486.6 × 365 = 53 days

Payables days = 79.8/190.4 × 365 = 153 days

This means that there is a difference of 100 days between receiving payment from customers and paying creditors. This reveals good management of cash flow.

In 2014, receivables days was 46 days and payables days was 124 days, a difference of 78 days. In terms of financial efficiency, the business has improved. This will please shareholders as it shows that Superdry should not encounter any cash-flow problems. The only possible concern is that Superdry is taking longer to pay its creditors. This may upset some of its suppliers who in future may demand quicker payment.

In conclusion, shareholders should be pleased with Superdry's financial performance. The business has achieved improved profitability and cash-flow management in 2015.

@ **16/16 marks awarded.** This answer reveals good understanding of both profitability and financial efficiency. Appropriate ratios are chosen and all calculations are correct. The analysis includes a comparison with the 2014 figures and provides effective explanation of why shareholders would be pleased.

The conclusion directly answers the question and is supported by the previous arguments.

Student B

In 2015, the ROCE for Superdry was 18%. This is better than the 15.3% in 2014 so shareholders will be pleased because the company is making more profit.

The payables days in 2015 was 153 days compared with 124 days in 2014. This means that Superdry is taking longer to pay its bills. This could upset its suppliers.

The receivables days for 2015 was 51 days compared with 46 days in 2014. This means that customers are taking longer to pay their bills. Because of this Superdry could have problems with cash flow.

Shareholders will be happy with the increase in profits but worried about longer payables and receivables days.

@ **7/16 marks awarded.** This answer shows understanding of profitability and financial efficiency by using correct ratios. It makes the mistake of not showing how the calculations were performed. This is particularly important as the calculation for receivables days is incorrect. Consequently, it is difficult to see where the calculation error was made.

There is limited analysis of the calculations and no attempt to compare the difference between payables and receivables days for each year.

The conclusion does answer the question but is supported by only limited analysis.

Question 3

Superdry has adopted a strategic position in its market by offering products that appeal to customers who are interested in stylish clothes of good quality priced higher than the average. What do you think is the biggest influence on this strategic position?

(20 marks)

e This type of question requires you to consider the different influences on a particular decision and then, in your conclusion, decide which is the most important. You do not need to identify several influences. Usually a maximum of three, each of which must be well analysed and illustrated with relevant information from the case study, would be sufficient.

Student A

Strategic positioning is the decision made by senior management regarding how the business will try to differentiate itself from its rivals in terms of its image. Michael Porter recommends that a business should either position itself as the lowest-cost producer or adopt a differentiation strategy by offering superior quality.

Superdry has adopted a differentiation position by offering stylish clothes of good quality that are priced higher than the average. One key influence on this position is Superdry's competitors. Companies such as Primark have been very successful as low-cost producers, meaning that customers are attracted by low prices. Superdry would find it difficult to compete with Primark, so has adopted a market position based upon quality rather than price.

Another influence would be the target market. Superdry's customers 'come from a broad background, are aspirational and interested in both style and quality'. Although the business was successful at first with 20–24-year-old men, it is now aiming at other age groups. For example, its customer profile reveals that 40% of its customers are aged 20–24, 35% are 25–34 and 25% aged over 35. It also says that its customers are 'aspirational'. This means that it appeals to customers who like to be seen as successful. 90% of its customers are either high or middle income, meaning that they can afford Superdry's higher than average prices.

Another influence would be the skills of its workforce. Superdry needs to have talented designers who are able to come up with new ideas for stylish clothing. It also needs employees in its stores who are able to offer the high levels of service that its customers would expect. If Superdry was unable to consistently achieve this, it would find it difficult to maintain its market position.

In conclusion, I think the biggest influence on Superdry's market position is its target market. The business wants to achieve sustainable long-term growth and this is dependent upon attracting high- and middle-income customers from a broad age group. As long as this market remains large enough and Superdry can gain high levels of brand loyalty from its target customers, its market position of differentiation is the correct one.

ⓔ 20/20 marks awarded. This answer reveals good understanding of market positioning by referring to Michael Porter's theory.

It identifies three relevant influences on Superdry's market position, each of which is well explained and illustrated with relevant examples from the case study.

The conclusion directly answers the question and is supported by the previous arguments.

Student B

A market position is how a business tries to make itself different from its competitors. Superdry offers products that are stylish and of good quality rather than having low prices.

One reason why it has done this is because it gives it an advantage over its competitors. If it offers more fashionable clothes, Superdry will get a good reputation and attract more customers.

Another reason why it has adopted this position is that it will attract wealthier customers who can afford to pay higher prices. This means the business can make more profit.

Another reason is the economy. If the economy is doing well, customers have more money to spend. This means that they can afford to buy the better quality Superdry products rather than the cheap ones sold by Primark.

Another reason is consumer tastes and fashions. If Superdry can bring out new products like the Idris Elba collection, it can attract customers who like Idris Elba and want to wear the same clothes that he does.

Overall I would say that the biggest influence is customers. This is because if Superdry does not offer fashionable, good-quality clothes, customers will go to its competitors like Abercrombie and Fitch instead.

ⓔ 8/20 marks awarded. This answer shows some understanding of market positioning but fails to make sufficient use of relevant theory.

It identifies relevant influences such as customers and competitors, but does not directly answer the question. This is because the answer explains the benefits Superdry has gained from its market position of differentiation, rather than the influences on why it decided to adopt this market position.

Each point is also not sufficiently developed. Fewer points with fuller analysis and application would have produced a better answer.

The conclusion attempts to answer the question but would be considered as only limited evaluation because it is not supported by sufficient previous analysis.

Knowledge check answers

1 Improve profitability, become the market leader, diversification into new markets.
2 Specific, Measurable, Agreed, Realistic, Time related.
3 Strategic: investment in new automated production systems. Tactical: staff training on new machinery.
4 Finance: maintain good cash flow.
Marketing: increase sales revenue of existing products.
Operations: reduce the number of defective products.
Human resources: reduce labour turnover.
5 Advantage: it enables a business to assess its current position and its future potential.
Disadvantage: it can be time consuming and consequently less useful in fast-changing markets.
6 Shareholders: potential dividends/effect on the share price.
Employees: job security/effect on pay and conditions.
Suppliers: stability and liquidity of the business in terms of receiving payment.
7 Non-current assets, such as machinery and buildings, are used by a business for longer than 1 year.
Current assets, for example inventories, are used for less than 1 year.
8 Cost of sales represents the direct costs of a business such as inventories and production workers' wages.
9 Overheads are the indirect costs of a business, such as rent and administration.
10 Financing costs are the borrowing costs of a business, such as interest payments on loans.
11 Machinery, IT systems, staff training.
12 Operating profit = gross profit – expenses.
Capital employed = non-current liabilities + total equity (shareholders funds).
13 Current asset: inventories, receivables, cash.
Current liability: overdraft, payables, tax.
14 Less money has been raised from shareholders, meaning that the business is under less pressure to provide high dividend payments.
15 Sales promotion, e.g. price discounts to attract customers.
16 Better credit control to ensure that customers pay on time.
17 The business may gain a bad reputation, resulting in difficulties in gaining contracts with existing and new suppliers.
18 To make the business appear to be worth more than it actually is.
19 Market share $= \dfrac{\text{sales of one product or business}}{\text{total market sales}} \times 100$

20 The number of 'hits' on the website, 'likes' on Facebook, 'followers' on Twitter.
21 Labour turnover $= \dfrac{\text{number of employees leaving during a given period}}{\text{total number of employees during a given period}} \times 100$
Labour productivity $= \dfrac{\text{total output}}{\text{number of employees}}$
22 Increased productivity, better quality and improved customer service.
23 Capacity utilisation $= \dfrac{\text{actual output}}{\text{maximum possible output}} \times 100$
24 Improved efficiency and quality should result in lower unit costs. This could enable the business to generate higher operating profit from its capital employed.
25 Innovation resulting from the employment of skilled software developers and product designers combined with talented marketing employees.
26 Lack of retained profits for investment may affect the long-term success of the business.
27 Increased retained profits for investment may result in lower dividend payments and a fall in the share price.
28 Examples of social/environmental costs include pollution and road congestion. Social/environmental benefits include the creation of secure jobs by socially responsible businesses and the development of green energy such as solar and wind power.
29 More competitive prices, improved customer service and the development of new products and services.
30 Improved morale, less absenteeism and lower labour turnover.
31 Cost: investment in waste treatment equipment. Benefit: lower waste treatment costs.
32 Job creation, economic wealth and increased competition.
33 To ensure that suppliers are able to deliver when required without delays.
34 Cheaper clothing, trainers and electrical goods, for instance.
35 Strategically, to ensure that the UK is not dependent upon imports for certain essential products and services. To protect developing industries from more powerful foreign competition.
36 Rise in demand for more expensive products/ services, e.g. BMW cars.
Fall in demand for inferior goods, e.g. poundshops.
No significant change in demand for normal goods such as groceries, e.g. Tesco.
37 Consumers with mortgages may benefit from lower monthly payments providing them with rising disposable incomes.
38 UK holidays will be cheaper for foreign customers, resulting in more sales.

39 An increase in labour productivity, which should result in lower unit costs.

40 To prevent large-scale unemployment.

To protect suppliers that are dependent upon the steel industry from going out of business.

41 Access to a huge market.

Diversification into a new market.

Lower production and transport costs.

42 Large available workforce.

Lower labour costs than in Western economies, e.g. Europe, the USA.

Greater economic wealth resulting in increased demand from Chinese consumers for 'Western' goods.

43 Social costs could include increased congestion and demand for services such as housing, education and health.

44 Higher overheads from having more shops as well as higher employment costs from needing a bigger workforce, resulting in higher prices.

45 Examples could include Innocent Drinks, the Co-operative Group and Marks and Spencer.

46 Employees may feel unfairly treated and customers may be charged higher prices.

47 Database to record customer purchases and tastes.

Using social media as a means of promotion.

Targeting customers directly through email and text messages.

48 Barriers to entry would be high due to the significant research and development as well as marketing costs required to compete with powerful rivals such as Sony and Microsoft.

49 Purchasing flights direct from airlines.

Using online operators such as Expedia and Lastminute.com.

Arranging accommodation independently using businesses such as Air BnB or Holiday Lettings.

50 Payback = number of complete years +

$$\frac{\text{amount still to be payed back}}{\text{total return in the year}} \times 12^*$$

* when calculating in a fraction of a month

Average rate of return =

$$\frac{\text{total net return/number of years}}{\text{initial cost}} \times 100$$

Net present value = total of present values – initial cost

51 Unexpected increases in costs, lower than expected returns due to new competition and/or economic recession.

52 May affect investment appraisal calculations as well as expected profit and breakeven figures.

53 Low initial prices, free connections and/or boxes, e.g. Virgin 'Tivo'.

54 At the time of writing: updated existing product – iPhone 6

New product – Fitbit Blaze watch

55 Clothing: Primark   Airlines: Ryanair

56 Car: BMW   Technology: Apple

57 High-quality materials, employing famous designers, selling only in exclusive stores.

58 Selling a range of more 'upmarket' foods such as lobster.

Weekly promotions on certain products that are not usually sold, for instance skiwear.

59 Expertise of the employees.

Competitors such as Samsung and Lenovo.

60 Constant innovation.

Maintaining a strong brand image.

Ensuring consistently high quality.

Note: Page numbers in **bold** indicate key terms.

Index